Raising Chickens for Beginners

A Step-by-Step Guide to Raising Happy Backyard Chickens in as Little as 30 Days

Small Footprint Press

—

Table of Contents

Introduction

As children, many of us had a fascination with dinosaurs. You may not be aware that chickens are closely related to dinosaurs! According to Sataksig (2018), when 68-million-year-old DNA from a *Tyrannosaurus ex* was compared to the DNA of 21 modern animal species, the closest match was that of the chicken! It may seem surprising that chickens are closely related to dinosaurs, but think of them as a T-Rex third cousin separated by more than 100 million years.

Casting the compelling dinosaur connection aside, chickens have evolved into the hottest backyard hobby or business for the last decade. Every year, thousands of people are entering into the ownership and care of our fine feathered friends. Keeping chickens in your backyard is not a new concept, and at one time in our history, it was quite common. During the Great Depression, it was encouraged to keep backyard chickens because food was hard to come by. When a family kept backyard chickens, they had access to fresh eggs and could raise their own meat birds.

Going forward from this era, small corner mom and pop grocery stores began popping up and supplying clean, white eggs and fresh roasted chicken, eliminating the need for individuals to keep their own chickens.

The rebirth of the backyard chicken movement can be attributed to the new generation of people interested in the green movement and the ability to control how their animals are fed, cared for, and the satisfaction of raising your own animals.

If you've never had the privilege of sharing time with chickens, then you have been missing out. Chickens have distinct personalities, and once people realize how individualized they are, their chickens become beloved pets and are often bestowed with loving names that embrace their behaviors and personalities.

No matter how your interest began, chickens have a charming way of working their way into the lives of people who had never given them a second thought. Even if you have no bird interest or experience, you will likely at one point find yourself wondering how you ever got along without them!

The first time anyone sees a chicken up close, they are immediately taken by their plumage, and that is quickly followed by the variations between breeds, the size differences, and their soft clucks. People have the misconception that chickens are noisy, which is not true. Outside of some clucks, the only time you will hear hens are when they are laying eggs, being attacked by a predator, or something interesting has been introduced to the flock like a slice of watermelon to attack or even a mouse in the hen house. Yes, it's true, chickens do eat mice, and they are omnivores. Roosters, on the other hand, are extremely noisy and not just in the wee hours of dawn's first light, but all the livelong day.

Before the backyard resurgence of chicken owners, there never seemed to be much information on how to get started in chicken ownership, keep them safe, make sure they were fed well, or how to pick the best chickens for beginner flock owners. Now, with the chicken business booming, there are books, blogs, seminars, and chicken experts that work for feed companies where you can pose any question you might have and get an answer quickly. The bottom line is hens must be cared for if you want them to thrive and produce.

It doesn't matter if you just want a few hens to supply you with eggs or you want to start your own little egg empire. Everyone must start somewhere. Depending on your local competition, you will find that you have more buyers than eggs since the appeal of farm-fresh eggs has captured the attention of buyers. Many of them want the product of healthy, free-range hens that truly get to go out and run around on the grass as they were meant to.

Backyard poultry for eggs and meat has become very appealing, and we can understand why consumers like to know where their dinner comes from. Since the United States began to allow our chickens to get shipped to China for processing, we have been very particular about what brands we choose to bring home for the dinner table, and there is a definite advantage knowing that your meats have come from just a few miles away. It brings a smile to your face to pick up a dozen eggs and see the hens frolicking outside.

There have been many animal husbandry fads over the years, but many of those quickly fade from the limelight. However, chickens are different; they are not a fad. Chickens are less than just the allure of having your own little egg stand and more about having a closer relationship with nature, knowing where your food comes from, and appreciating all the little tidbits of information that you will learn through your exposure to chickens. The more you learn about chickens, the better understanding you will have regarding these quirky birds and nature.

As a company, Small Footprint Press is focused and determined on providing the best help possible. We want to make it easy for people to return to the land and live more sustainably for the long term.

We do this by doing in-depth research for all our books, with topics ranging from survival training to various self-sufficiency methods and prepping for disasters (natural or human-caused). We work our hardest to teach you how to care for the planet Earth and its inhabitants in the most holistic and mutually beneficial manners possible. Our team is made of dedicated and enthusiastic nature lovers, who altogether have over three decades of combined knowledge of outdoorsmanship and conservation. We can't wait to pass it all along to you.

Our goal is to help empower you to achieve the sustainable lifestyle that you want. Like you, we feel that giving back to our planet is crucial for our continued survival as a species. We whole-heartedly believe that being outdoors (in a sustainable manner) makes us humans happy, and we want to share that happiness with you as well.

Chicken Choices

There are so many stories about how people got initiated into the world of chickens. The tales run the gambit from adopting chicks from school science projects to dyed Easter chicks that end up in the animal shelter after the cuteness factor has worn off, but the best way is to do a little homework before you dive right in. If you are lucky, there may be a local breeder nearby. The first decision you will need to make is what your ultimate goal is. There are four main functions for chickens, and you will need to figure out which niche interests you the most. These functions are eggs, meat, show or breeding, or fun. There are no wrong choices, just what interests you the most.

Egg Chickens

We all are familiar with egg and their plain white eggs, but some chickens lay brown, deep pink, blue, green, and a couple of other shades of brown eggs specific to a chicken's breed. A hen will never change the color of the eggs she lays during her lifetime but check out some fun egg color facts below.

- White eggs will be white all the way through.

- Brown eggs will be white on the inside.

- Blue eggs will be blue on the inside.

- Green eggs will be green on the outside, but blue on the inside.

Meat Chickens

Meat chickens, commonly called broilers, are a chicken bred to be a quick grower, and the number one choice for meat birds is a White Rock and Cornish Cross hybrid chicken. There is a big difference between a stewing hen, a broiler, or a roaster, and you should decide which you choose to raise.

Showing and Breeding Chickens

Show and breeding chickens are often fancier breeds. If you are serious about showing your chickens in competition, there are a lot of details that you will need to learn. Often the size of the comb or the angle of a tail can be important. To expand your knowledge, you should become familiar with the American Poultry Association's *American Standard of Perfections* that pertains to your specialized breed. Go to some poultry shows so that you know what a good animal looks like. Showing requires knowledge of genetics, good management, and excellent nutrition to breed champion bloodlines.

Urban Chickens

The backyard or urban chicken is less likely to end up in a stew pot and more likely to receive a proper burial like any beloved pet. Most of these chickens, even well after they stop laying, will be kept as cherished members of the family.

Everyone has their own story on how they became interested in and started raising chickens. But even if you tried it and the first time wasn't a positive experience, take heart, because armed with our knowledge, you will excel at the coop life and be one of those folks that tell others all about your chickens even if you weren't asked. Remember that all the cool people raise tiny dinosaurs!

Chapter 1:
Everyone Should Raise Chickens

You know you own chickens when...you watch them play in the yard more than you watch TV.

–Unknown

Ever host Olympic donut jumping with your flock? No, seriously! String about three donuts on a cord and lower and raise it slightly just to test your hen's jumping ability. Just make sure they win the prize and don't tease them by making the goal unattainable.

According to Jerome Belanger (2010), there are about a billion chickens in the world at any given time. That's three and a half chickens for every single human on Earth.

Is everyone suited to raise chickens? Without a certain commitment to the welfare of your animals, we would say no. You need dedication to provide for any animal, and it doesn't matter if it is a chicken, a dog, or a goldfish. They all need freshwater, food, shelter, cleanliness, love, and devotion. Sharing your life with any animal is a 365 day responsibility. While there are plenty of super dedicated owners out there, you should always have a willing helper to cover your precious flock when you are unavailable.

Chickens do require daily attention because they still need to be fed and watered every day. You should at least give the girls a cursory glance to ensure that they are all still feeling and acting their best. You will always want to clean and sanitize your flock's feeders and waterers once a week, possibly more in warmer weather. You should also plan on cleaning their coop at least once a week, but if you take a few minutes each day, their coop will be easy to maintain. Utilizing this method, you might only have to perform a strip once a year.

Raising Your Own Flock Is Easier Than You Think!

Looking back over your family history, we are sure that someone in your family tree raised chickens. The only difference is that they probably were born into a farming family and already possessed experience without ever picking up a book.

How much do you need to know to raise chickens? Truthfully, it depends. Some breeds are easier to raise than others. Often, folks just get lucky and choose the heartiest and best egg producers without even realizing what they are doing. Just diving in is how many people get started, but some crave every bit of knowledge before delving into the ownership of their own little flock. People should know what's involved if chickens are right for them.

Be honest about your goals. Some get into chickens to make money, but if you are an urbanite with three or four hens, obviously, making money is not first and foremost in your mind. Your backyard chickens are going to lay the best eggs you have ever tasted.

You may just want a small flock to provide eggs and meat for your family. As a backyard operation, you will certainly be able to provide more than enough eggs for your immediate family. Keep in mind that the majority of chicken owners don't raise them for meat since butchering is seldom allowed within the city or suburban limits. If your dream is to raise and slaughter meat birds, you had best check all the rules and regulations governing your area before you get your heart set on a new venture.

Why Chickens?

Many people want a greener lifestyle and buy a large portion of their food locally, but what could be more local than your own backyard? Perhaps you already planted a substantial garden full of fabulous vegetables, and you may even keep bees, so why not add chickens and their eggs to your little slice of heaven?

Even though the push to be green may have initiated the growth of urban backyard poultry owners, urbanites have kept their chickens for a multitude of reasons.

There is no stereotypical person that will choose to keep chickens, and most of them will have nothing in common with other chicken owners except for their flocks. Whether you keep chickens for pets, eggs, insect control, education, meat, composting, or fertilizer production, you are, without a doubt, a crazy chicken lady or man (that is a compliment, by the way).

We have already mentioned that chickens are entertaining, and there is nothing better than pulling up a chair and watching your girls catch bugs or take part in a dust bath. With too many stresses that take over our lives, it can be satisfying to relax and watch nature at its finest.

Reasons to Raise Chickens

As if people need reasons to keep chickens! But if you insist…

Some chickens have silky feathers, frizzled tops, feathers growing on their feet, or they might even sport a spiked look that would make the best punk-rockers jealous. The point is that there is a chicken for everyone, so whether you pine for bantams or clamor for more traditional breeds, choosing your first chicken can be a difficult decision. The great thing is that you do not have to decide on just one breed since most flocks are mixed.

If you like eggs, this is a no-brainer, but some people raise certain chickens for meat, shows, or just plain old entertainment and companionship. If you only have a few birds, you probably fall into the entertainment category.

Eggs, Eggs, and More Eggs!

Once you have tasted fresh eggs from your chickens that have been enhanced by free-ranging and feeding decisions that you have made, you will have a tough time forcing yourself to buy eggs at the store. Their taste will be richer than their store-bought competition, and they will taste better simply because you and your girls have made this happen. How many people can brag that they collected eggs this morning in the PJs? People that use fresh eggs swear that their baked goods turn out lighter and fluffier, but it is up to you to do that comparison testing. Remember, you can't make a cake without breaking a few eggs!

According to Deborah Niemann (2013), research has proven that eggs produced by free-range chickens test lower in cholesterol and higher in vitamins and minerals than their mass-produced sister eggs. She went on to compare the eggs produced by pastured hens, finding that they will have four to six times more vitamin D, seven times more beta-carotene, three times more vitamin E, and twice the amount of Omega-3 fatty acids than their grocery store competition.

Fewer Bugs

Chickens do a remarkable job eating ticks, fleas, mosquitoes, flies, or any other bug dumb enough to cross into a chicken's territory. Chickens not only eat the bugs but their larvae as well, so there will be fewer bugs being born on your property.

Preserve Important Chicken Breeds

Yes, you heard that right. Just like GMO-raised crops, the large factory farms utilize a breed of hybrid chicken that is designed to eat less, produce more and larger eggs, and do it all from a small crate-like box. Without the backyard hobbyist, certain breeds of chickens could become extinct.

Local Food Production

It can be refreshing to enjoy something that you only had to travel to the backyard to retrieve instead of a product that may have traveled up to 1,500 miles just to get to your local grocery store.

Pet Chickens!

Perhaps you aren't a dog, cat, or small rodent fan, but your kids really want a pet. The good news is chickens can double as a pet! Chickens are intelligent, trainable, and most breeds, when handled daily after hatching, will be friendly. If you do have other pets, rest assured your chickens will clean up all those nasty ticks, and your dog or cat won't suffer from that either. Your children can work on their mathematical abilities by counting eggs or working out how long a 50-pound bag of feed will last for your flock. Chickens can become very attached and will come running if they hear their names and know that you have treats for them.

Anti-GMO

If you are anti-GMO, then you are probably aware that caged hens are fed a diet consisting of GMO crops like corn, soy, and cottonseed meals. When you have control over what feeds your girls consume, then you can rest easy.

Chickens Provide You With Free Fertilizer

Imagine going to your local farm or garden center to *buy* chicken poop! If you have a garden, your chicken's manure will be a great addition to the soil.

Chicken TV

Free entertainment can be had by watching your chicken's antics. Besides watching your first egg being laid, it can be pretty entertaining to watch your girls corner a mouse. You can also give them plenty of fruits and veggies that may be past their prime for you to eat. Hens make pretty short work of cantaloupes and stale popcorn as well.

Cruelty-Free

You know for a fact that your girls are well cared for and happy. You may believe that you are currently buying cruelty-free eggs already, but you should be aware that what those egg cartons say and what it really means can be two different things. For example, when you see a carton that is stamped "free-range," there is no actual defined description of what that is. It may conjure scenes of hens frolicking in meadows, but less than one percent of chickens in the United States are considered to be free-range. Some wording to be aware of is found below.

- "All-natural." Sure, it sounds appealing, but it promises you nothing other than it's a real egg from a real hen.

- "Cage-free" doesn't mean cruelty-free. Simply put, these hens are given the freedom to be out of restrictive cages; that much is true. However, what these hens have been given is access to roam a facility, but that doesn't mean that they are enjoying the great outdoors.

- "Free-range" adds a step to cage-free by allowing hens to live in or are able to get access to outdoors.

- "Farm fresh." Yep, sorry, that is also a marketing ploy. What it really means is that you are buying an egg from a hen that is kept on a commercial farm.

- "Organic" eggs come only from free-range hens. To be certified organic, these hens must be fed only organic feed, and nothing labeled poultry by-products, antibiotics, any animal drugs, or manure.

- "No hormones" isn't ground-breaking since no egg-laying hens found in the US are allowed to receive hormones.

- An "Omega-3" label doesn't instantly mean that those eggs contain proven levels of this important fatty acid. Hens that lay Omega-3 branded eggs can only eat feed that contains flaxseed.

- "Vegetarian diet." Nope. Remember when you read our introduction and found out that the chicken is related to the T-rex through DNA? Well, Tyrannosaurus Rex surely wasn't vegan, and neither are chickens. That's right, chickens are omnivores and enjoy the occasional small animal, like frogs and mice, in addition to their plants, bugs, and spiders. They will even eat cooked chicken! When chickens are forced to follow a vegetarian diet, they can fall ill and even start pecking at each other. Depriving your hens of the needed amino acid, methionine, will cause them to become sickly.

- "Pasture-raised" hens mean that those hens have spent their lives or parts of them at least with access to a pasture. This also means that they have been allowed to forage naturally supplementing facility-provided foods. Unfortunately, there are no standards for the pasture or what the facility believes constitutes a pasture. No inspections for pasture-raised are presently required. These terms can be a real eye-opener, can't they?

Educational Lessons for You and Your Children to Share

Were you aware that chickens have a great memory? Hens are a tight-knit community that enjoy playing. They dream, feel pain, distress, mourn for each other, and they also make excellent mothers. Hens talk to their chicks while still in the confines of the egg, and they will turn their eggs about 50 times each day. Your hens will follow a social structure based on a determined hierarchy, or if you prefer, "pecking order." By keeping chickens, your children can learn about nature, math, agriculture, and the responsibility of caring for living creatures.

Chickens Eat Food Scraps

Want to cut down on food scraps that you send to the local landfill? Your chickens can eat most kitchen scraps, including fruit and vegetable peelings, bread, cooked beans, cooked rice, pasta, oatmeal, and more.

Weed Control

While they can be good at weed control, they will also pick your flower bed and garden clean, so cleaning up the weeds might be best when left for after the growing season. At that point, you can turn the girls loose, and they can eat all the leftover veggies you declined to eat and drop some fertilizer in there for the next growing year.

Chickens for Therapy?

Chickens are being viewed as therapeutic for the elderly and children suffering from autism. Because chickens are always on the move and socializing within the flock, they have been found to calm patients suffering from dementia and other psychiatric disorders.

Owning Chickens can Open Social Doors

Want to share your newfound passion with others? Look no further than a quick internet search to find similar-minded chicken owners full of their newfound passion and ready to share their tips and helpful suggestions.

It's a Fun Hobby

Some people may not be able to understand your chicken passion, but then again, personally, we find coin collecting tedious. To each his own!

It's Relatively Inexpensive

Yes, there are startup costs, but once you have built your dream coop that keeps your flock safe, you will only need food, bedding, and a few pieces of equipment.

Chicks, Pullets, or Full-Grown Chickens?

Even if you have settled on one choice, you may be limited by what's available at the time. Traditionally, chicks are hatched in the spring, so there is a small window of opportunity to make your livestock purchase. Most young hens, or pullets, are mostly available in summer and fall. There was a time when chickens of this age weren't even an option to purchase, but there have been some visionaries that started raising their chicks to sell as pullets, but these sellers might be hard to find. Your best bet is to plan on starting with chicks in spring or early summer.

You can go online and contact some of the hatcheries for their catalogs. This is an excellent way of learning more about the different breeds. The majority of people get their first chickens via mail-order.

So, What's a Bantam?

A bantam is just a small chicken or a smaller version of a bigger chicken. These fun little birds usually weigh no more than two pounds and are about one-fourth the size of an average chicken. Because of their size, they don't eat much, make great pets, and they tolerate confinement well. They will almost always have a personality that is bigger than life.

Almost every chicken breed has a bantam counterpart, but there are some breeds that are only available in the bantam size. These birds are popular to show because they are easy to handle.

Chapter 2:
What Makes Your Chickens Happy?

The oldest chicken to have ever lived was a Red Quill Muffed American Gamebird named Muffy. Well cared for chickens typically live 7 to 8 years, but miracle Muffy lived until she was 22 years old. She must have been happy indeed!

— Unknown

All living creatures yearn to belong socially, feel love, and enjoy freedom; your chickens are no different. There is nothing wrong with showing your chickens that they are special and a part of the family. They have the same intelligence as your family dog or cat, so why not extend your sentiments to your family chickens? Your flock wants to be loved and cared for, and here are some pointers to make them feel special.

- **Never keep a solitary chicken**. Probably *the* most important thing to remember is that chickens are not solitary souls. They like to socialize with others of their own kind and need to in order to be happy and healthy. We recommend no less than three chickens as a bare minimum. If you only get two, but one is killed by a predator, then you are going to have one lonely, depressed chicken!

- **Call to your flock.** By announcing your arrival, especially at dinner time, your chickens will recognize that food is *en route*, and you are the bringer of the said feast. When they hear you call out to them, they will come running because they have learned to associate you with food and treats. Who doesn't enjoy those? You can make their favorite treat something you provide at bedtime as an encouragement to return to the coop for the night. For example, cracked corn can be used to entice them in for the night or out in another area while you clean up their coop.

- **Spoil them with live or freeze-dried mealworms.** Nothing will bring your hens running and cackling quicker than a tasty mealworm. Sit back and watch them enjoy pecking apart a squash, pumpkin, or watermelon.

- **Spend some time with your flock.** Just as you would pay attention to your dog or cat, simply sit and visit with them. Plop down in a lawn chair in their pasture or sit in their coop, so they become acclimated to your presence. Take care to not sit in too tall of a chair so that you seem to tower over them. It doesn't matter if you watch them, read a book, or watch a movie on your phone. Just being around them without trying to catch them will calm any flighty hens you might have. You can even toss some treats out around your chair. We can guarantee you that if you appear uninterested in them, they will pester you for your attention. The more you can do this, the quicker your hens will bond with you.

- **Always move slowly.** Birds are easily frightened by quick movements. Resist any urges to run, jump, or move quickly around them. If you hold a chicken too tightly, they will start to panic, so take care to hold them in a supportive but unrestricted way. Take care, especially with a rooster if you have one; they have been known to attack the eyes of their human handlers when too close to a human face.

- **Know your rooster well.** If you are breeding, you want to use only the cuddly roosters. Aggression has no place in a flock of chickens.

- **Approach chicks carefully.** Baby chicks experience a whole new level of nervousness because, let's face it, they are tiny and afraid of everything. When you stand over them, they see you as a predator until you can build their trust level. The best way is to try and keep yourself at their level as much as possible.

- **Chickens will respond to gentle handling.** If you have smaller children that handle the birds, you should teach them proper ways to handle chickens, especially young chicks. When your chicks are content, they will spread out in the brooder and move around practicing their scratching, eating, drinking, and cuddling under the light to sleep. You will hear them emit happy, quiet chirps when content.

- **Toys!** Believe it or not, your flock loves to play with stuff. Chickens need physical and mental stimulation that will keep them entertained. If you don't believe me, just add a chicken swing or a chicken ladder and watch the antics that this causes. There are pre-made swings, but also tutorials on making one if you feel that you are a handy person. Your flock will also find loads of entertainment playing with old tree stumps or hollowed-out stumps, unbreakable mirrors, old balls, or even a low-hanging cabbage.

Chickens Like Their Space

Chickens need room to roam. It is very important to make sure that you have given your chickens enough space, if you will forgive the expression, to spread their wings. This is a vital piece needed to keep your flock happy and content.

How much room you need to allow for your new hobby is going to hinge on how many chickens you plan on adding to the family. You would never want to have less than three or four chickens, so let's plan on using the average of six to get started. You should take into account that your chickens will be kept in a coop at nighttime and given free rein to roam during the daylight hours. A coop for six chickens would need a bare minimum of 18 square feet with a run of around 90 square feet. When you combine these, you should have right around 110 square feet to keep six chickens.

We can almost hear the wheels turning in your head. You're thinking that bigger is better, and your six chickens are going to be given the Taj Mahal of coops with tons of room to roost and nest. If you live in a warm climate, you can probably get away with that, but if you are living in a colder climate, your six chickens are going to have difficulty generating enough heat to keep their coop warm.

Allowing your chickens to roam is one of the easiest ways to provide your chickens with sun-filled afternoons spent chasing bugs in the pasture. They can forage for themselves and claim healthy greens, bugs, and the occasional small rodent or two. Depending upon where you live, your chickens may even score a few scorpions or tarantulas (funny story on tarantulas later)! If you don't want them running free all day, you can easily schedule them for an hour in the morning and evening, allowing you the ability to watch them. Whatever routine you set for them, you will find that they can get into the groove of a routine fairly quickly.

Besides providing your flock with their very own coop, you will need to add nesting boxes, so the girls will have a place to hang out and lay their eggs. You can purchase individual plastic nesting boxes online or from specialty stores. You can also build a sectioned nesting box. Another option, and one some of our friends have chosen, is to use an old piece of vintage furniture that has some sections already in place and tear off the backer while placing this in a cut-out area of your coop with the doors facing out. This will allow your chickens to nest, and you can just open the doors from the other side to collect the eggs. The first time we saw this, we thought it was brilliant. If you are in a hurry to quickly collect eggs mid-afternoon, then you don't even have to enter the coop part. No matter how you choose to set up your nesting boxes, they should be about a square foot per chicken (they may need to be larger if you have chosen a larger breed).

Outside for a breath of fresh air and sunshine, your basic six chickens will need about 90 square feet (6 x 15). This isn't a large piece of land when you think about it, and an area of grass that is roughly 10 x 10 is adequate, but if you want happy hens, the more room you can give them, the better. Where you allow your chickens to roam is completely up to you. Whether you choose a portable run, create a permanent run, or just allow them free-roaming rights, this is all a very personal choice, and each has its advantages and disadvantages. The bigger the space, the more exciting their days will be.

Your free-range chickens are going to be given more space than their commercial counterparts. Remember that the US Department of Agriculture states that a free-range chicken should have access to the outside, but there are no rules governing how much space they are allowed or for how long they need to remain outside to qualify for this description.

Keep it Clean!

Keep their coop clean. This may seem a bit daunting at first since chickens poop *everywhere*, but that doesn't mean that they enjoy being dirty or living in filth.

An advantage to frequent cleaning, besides happy, healthy hens, is your familiarity with the condition of the coop. Coops will need repairs from time to time, so in order to keep your flock safe, you should pay close attention to any areas that might need fixing.

A clean coop will keep your flock healthy by preventing diseases. Should you have nearby neighbors, they too will thank you for keeping the smell at a minimum.

To have a tidy coop, we recommend you clean every day (during the winter twice a day, if they are kept inside). By keeping on top of the mess, especially in the winter, you can quickly flip droppings into a dustpan with a paint scraper and then empty the dustpan into an empty feed bag. You can then either compost it outside or, if you have too much compost, just dispose of it. We still love the deep bedding method, and you can also strip and rebed twice a year. We'd love for your coop to sparkle!

The middle-of-the-road approach is to clean the coop once a week and do spot cleaning every other day. If you have hens that like to sleep in the nesting boxes, then there will be a lot of poop in those nests, and they will need to be cleaned out daily. If you stay ahead of the mess, it will save you time when you do a complete cleanout, and you only need to allow 15 minutes or so each time you clean.

Many people like the deep litter method, which is simply adding materials to the coop floor, allowing the waste to compost inside the coop. Then a few times a year, they will strip and rebed the entire coop, scooping all the waste into the garden.

No matter what method you decide to use, you should always level out the bedding, so there are no bare spaces. If you think the levels seem a bit low, you can always add more bedding to the floor of the coop.

When setting up your food and water areas, you should take care to keep them far away from any roosting bars or nesting boxes. We like to use a hanging feed and water container so that they cannot poop in it. You should also be taking these down and cleaning them out regularly to wash away any dirt and prevent anything disgusting from growing inside.

If you don't keep your nesting boxes clean and tidy, your hens may stop laying. If you keep on top of it, the process won't take long. Regularly remove all the bedding and simply replace it with fresh nesting materials. There are several different materials that you can use for nesting, including shredded paper, hay, pine or cedar shavings, straw, or some people even use mulch.

Chickens like to roost. It's hardwired into their instinct, and they prefer to choose elevated roosts to avoid predators. A roost can be an elevated branch or plank on which your chickens can perch to sleep. Your provided roosting perch will be a place where your birds will stay all night, keeping the balance of their flock all around them. As an added value in the winter, they will be able to keep warmer. Ideally, your roosting perch should be around 1.5 to three feet high. When you are planning your roosts, you may want to consider a small, lower perch just for those older arthritic hens. Heavier birds, like an Orpington or a Jersey Giant, might benefit from lower perches as well because larger birds are more prone to get leg injuries. When you choose your breeds, you may want to configure your roosts to take their individual needs in mind.

Your roosting bars will need to be kept clean because chickens will still poop on them. Our personal favorite tool to clean perches is a garden hoe. If you run this garden tool over the bars, you can knock off all the poop, and if necessary, the bar can be sprayed down with a water hose to remove any lingering poop. You can provide some sanitizing to the bar by soaking a sponge in white vinegar and running this over the bars.

Never Underestimate the Power of a Good Dust Bath!

After a long, hard day of working outside, we love nothing better than hopping in the shower to wash away our daily dose of dirt. We need to understand that chickens don't bathe as we do, and it may seem counterintuitive, but chickens get clean by getting dirty. Yes, we are sure that you have reread that last sentence a couple of times, and you are probably shaking your head thinking that it doesn't make any sense, but hear us out.

All chickens need dust baths, and it is a natural behavior. They will dig a shallow pit by choosing the finest, most irritating dust that they can find. We bet that you are dying to know why they roll around in it until they have covered every possible area of skin and feather. It's because it keeps the parasites away. Yep, mites and lice find all this dust to be irritating, so oddly enough, all that fine silty sand, dust, or ashes are appropriate materials to supply for your chicken's dust bath.

Your girls will probably make this a social event that will involve everyone in the flock, and you may witness a community event. These dust baths aren't just for chickens alone. Should you have a mixed flock with some added turkeys or quail, they will also enjoy the benefits of the dust bath.

Will your chickens use a dust bath in the winter? Yes, but not as often, since lice and mites are less of a problem during colder months. Your chickens should have something to use year-round.

The area for a dust bath needs to be big enough for a hen, but if they have a dust bath party, it should be big enough for several hens to flop around comfortably. If you are trying to design your own area, you should take the number of birds you have into consideration. The dust bath for the average size chickens should be around eight inches deep and only six inches if you are raising bantams. The rule of thumb is that they should be deep enough to fit a chicken.

Your chickens will probably decide on the perfect place for a dust bath, but the area should be a dry, covered area that your chickens will have easy access to. If you don't provide one, they will most likely make one in your favorite flowerpot! Even if you believe you have created the best dust bath area, your hens may just pick out a spot and plop down. We guess as long as they are happy, that's all that matters.

So, what are some materials that you can provide for your chicken's bath *du jour*? The bulk of it can be just clean, dry, sand, but here are some other alternatives you can add.

- Charred wood or fire ash from a wood fire. Some chickens will even pick charcoal out from the ash you provide and consume it. It is believed that this helps to absorb any toxins residing in their gut.

- Diatomaceous earth, commonly known as DE. A little goes a long way, but a super fine grade of DE will kill lice, mites, and other parasites just by contact. There is some debate on the use of DE. See below in supplements.

- They will not appreciate a bubble bath, but you can provide them with some nice, dried herbs in their dustbowls, and many of these also provide protection from pests. Try some lavender, lemon balm, mint, rosemary, or sage. If you are growing your own herb garden, you will have these readily available.

- Sawdust can be used, but make sure that they are not camphor or heavily fragrant.

- Topsoil. Chickens love to toss loose dirt over themselves, and even if you buy a bag of topsoil at your home improvement store, it doesn't cost much to make your hens happy.

Avoid adding any of these to the dust bath area.

- Straw. The hollow nature of straw is an excellent hiding place for lice, mites, and mold. These are the very things your hens are trying to avoid.

- Coal ash can contain mercury, sulfur, and heavy metals.

- Kitty litter is often manufactured to include fragrances and deodorizers.

- Fire log ash is a product of commercially compressed logs or pellets. In the industry, they grind up many things like wood, adhesives, varnishes, stains, and added glue. They may even use old pallets that housed who knows what. It would be risky to expose your birds to potentially harmful chemicals.

A Fed Chicken Is a Happy Chicken

Well, every animal enjoys eating, but giving them a good quality feed will keep their insides healthy, which in turn will keep them happy. If you remember that you are eating their eggs, it isn't too difficult to rationalize that the better the food, the better the egg. So, keeping their tummies happy in turn keeps ours happy as well.

Freshwater is a given for every living creature, but sometimes it can be a challenge with chickens. If you provide a dish on the floor, you can expect to not only see them stand in it but poop in it as well. Our personal favorite is a bucket that has nipples and a lid that you can hang from a support system. Not only will this keep your chickens from soiling the water, but it will keep pests out of it too. Just remember to freshen the water at least once each day.

Keep their environment safe. We all feel happier knowing that we are safe and secure. Your coop should be free from pests and predators, which can include the family cat or dog. If you have other family pets that enjoy chasing your chickens, this will stress out your girls, and they may either stop laying eggs or hide them.

Supplements & Herbs

Supplements are fed in addition to your feed. Some of our personal favorites are garlic, apple cider vinegar, and diatomaceous earth. If your flock indulges in a lot of free-range time, they shouldn't need any supplements.

Garlic

Garlic is a natural antibiotic and can strengthen your chicken's immune system while also boosting its respiratory system. Garlic is a natural deterrent for lice and mites and is an active ingredient in natural dewormers. You might be wondering how to give your chickens garlic, and there are a few methods. We prefer to crush bulbs and mince them, then offer it as a treat by itself or mixed with other treats. There are some that prefer to add powdered garlic to their feed, but there have been some arguments that this method is not as powerful as giving fresh, raw garlic. This is not something you need to provide for your flock daily, once or twice a month is perfectly adequate. Overfeeding could cause your birds to be unable to balance the bacteria in their digestive system. Of course, only feed organic garlic!

Organic Apple Cider Vinegar

Organic apple cider vinegar (ACV), for example, Braggs, which is known for its quality and benefit of "the mother," can help your chickens with their immunity, improve their overall health, help optimize digestive health, and help a chick get over the sour crop (see chapter 4). The best way to dispense ACV to your chickens is to add a single tablespoon to every gallon of freshwater. **Note that ACV should not be administered in any metal water dispenser!** This should be offered to your flock 1 to 2 times a week.

Diatomaceous Earth (DE)

Diatomaceous earth is debated by chicken owners; some feel that it is safe, while others believe it to be a health hazard. All we can tell you is that there are benefits and risks. The ultimate decision is yours. DE is a natural substance made from fossils of microscopic aquatic algae, called diatoms. This mined substance is ground into a fine powder, but these fossilized diatoms are made up of almost pure amorphous silicon. The reason this is important to know is that this is a crystalline form of silica, which can cause silicosis (a form of lung cancer).

In the US, a product that is less than 2% crystalline silica is considered safe. However, when you compare that to other countries' standards, that is considered to be high. While this is effective against external parasites, such as red mites, northern fowl mites, fleas, and lice, there are other, more safe alternatives to use. The main concern of this product revolves around the risk of breathing in the dust. Diatomaceous earth is a dusty powder that, even if you handle it with care, can fly everywhere.

You can grow an herb garden for your flock! Some herbs help with your chicken's health and well-being below. We have listed some of the more popular herbs and how they help:

- **Chamomile** can be a wonderful addition to your chicken's supplements. It can be used in your flock's fight against lice, mites, and fleas. Chamomile is also well known for its calming properties, and chickens are no exception.

- **Chives** provide an excellent source of iron for your flock and, in addition, can help with digestion.

- **Cilantro** is believed to help build strong bones, aid in vision, and act as a fungicide.

- **Dandelion** is good for the overall health of your chickens, and if you are an urban farmer that is dedicated to improving the Earth, you probably have an abundance of these. People actually used to plant dandelions! For a greener earth, we need to embrace these gifts from nature.

- **Dill** helps with your flocks' digestion, respiratory health, and appetite. It also serves as an antioxidant.

- **Lavender** not only smells great but can help your chickens reduce their stress. And if placed in the nests, lavender can help repel insects.

- **Lemon Balm** helps reduce stress, is antibacterial, and can help reduce pests.

- **Marigold** can help keep bugs away, aids your hens to produce more orange yolks, and promotes healthy beaks and feet.

- **Mint** is always a favorite staple of any herb garden because of its ability to keep mice away and bugs too. Mint has been said to increase your hen's egg production and overall eggshell quality.

- **Nasturtium** is a nice little flower, but while it isn't an herb, it can do some very impressive things besides repelling bugs! Nasturtiums work as a natural chicken dewormer and act as an antibiotic. It is also believed to aid in egg production.

- **Oregano** is a powerful antibiotic and a staple of any herb garden. Oregano can fight coccidia, salmonella, E. coli, avian flu, and helps to strengthen the chickens' immune systems.

- **Parsley** is always a highly undervalued herb but contains high levels of vitamins A, B, and C, along with high calcium and iron levels.

- **Rosemary** is another herb that bugs tend to hate, but it can also be used as a pain reliever and help out with respiratory health.

- **Sage** is great for the overall health of your birds and is believed to aid in fighting salmonella.

- **Thyme** can help our chickens fight parasites, stimulate laying, and promote healthy respiratory systems.

Chicken Behavior

Chickens are social creatures that establish their own "pecking order" and have developed their own language. Taking the time to understand your chicken's behavior can make your experience more interesting, rewarding, and infinitely more fun.

Let's delve into the social life of chickens to gain a better understanding of our feathered friends.

The Pecking Order

Almost everyone that has heard the term knows that it is closely associated with chickens. The term "pecking order" was first used to describe chickens in 1921, and it just sort of stuck. In the world of chickens, the inclusion in the pecking order begins at six to eight weeks of age. At this age, chickens will display signs of dominance, submissiveness, escape, avoidance, and attack. According to Jerome Belanger (2010), researchers have discovered that an individual chicken can recognize and remember more than a hundred other chickens!

Once a pecking order has been established within your flock, it is accepted as chicken law by all members, and there is peace throughout the chicken kingdom. In this hierarchy, every chicken will know its place. Chickens live in flocks similar to human communes. They share a communal approach when it comes to the raising of their young or the incubation of the flock's eggs.

While watching some of your lower-ranking chickens, you may notice that they will keep their heads lower than their more dominant flockmates. These lower-ranking chickens are monitored by their higher-ups, and if they slip and forget their place, they will be quickly reminded where they stand.

If your flock does have roosters, they will develop their own ranking and should demonstrate a passive dominance over the hens. After all, they are the protectors of the flock. Your hens will form their own order outside of the roosters, and interestingly, larger combs may award a hen with a higher rank.

When a new bird is introduced to your flock, it can cause chaos, and the hierarchy will have to be established all over again. A good rule of thumb is that if you must introduce new birds, you should not make it a frequent habit. Frequent changes can stress out your birds, which can lower their immunity and cause some of them to develop an illness or stop laying altogether.

Great care should be taken when introducing new members to your flock. It can be hard to believe that your contented flock can turn into a bunch of bullies when you try to add a new hen to the group, but it is possible. If you want happy chickens, you will need to be careful and considerate of your existing flock when you add new birds.

If you need to introduce a new chicken into your flock, it should take place gradually and, for some reason, more toward dusk. Your new chicken can be kept in a cage or crate where they can all meet and greet each other without any physical altercations. The acceptance of newcomers can vary from flock to flock because some chickens or breeds of chickens can be more socially acceptable than others.

We have a friend who swears by sneaking the new chicken in the coop while all the other chickens are sleeping and placing her on a roost. In her experience, the flock will wake up and not even care about the new addition. She says that it's like they wake up and think the new chicken has always been there. We have to admit, we haven't tried it.

You should also be aware that if you remove hens or roosters from the group, this will also add disruption to the flock, and a new pecking order will have to be put in place.

Want to Make a Difference?

You can adopt a former battery hen. Until recently, we weren't even aware of this ourselves, but you can help a once caged chicken to enjoy the creature comforts of your backyard's free-range offerings. A battery hen has never stepped foot outside of her cage, scratched through the dirt to find some delectable bug, nor even enjoyed a dust bath. These hens have never experienced freedom, and it can be a difficult transition for them while trying to adjust.

You will find that these hens have experienced years of trauma, and unfortunately, that isn't going to go away by spending an afternoon in your backyard chicken retreat. These girls have no idea how to perch or rest in a nesting box, so you have to give them time to adjust to a whole new world.

Having never enjoyed a moment of freedom, former battery hens may find themselves overwhelmed and even frightened by their new surroundings. As their new owner, you need to stay patient and keep calm because it is going to take them as long as it takes them to be at ease in a new world.

They are going to have a lot to learn since they have never had to worry about pecking orders, farm dogs, or exposure to alien noises. You will need to introduce them slowly to the flock, and above all, keep an eye on their health. Battery hens will have below-average resistance to diseases, and you should make it a top priority to have them given any necessary vaccinations they might need, treat them for worms, parasites, and coccidiosis, in addition to any other diseases you or your vet deem relevant.

As they begin to feel safe and are fed a healthy diet, they will start to grow back any feathers they may have lost due to their prior lifestyle. They may not have any eggs left at this point, but they can still make gentle pets if you just give them a chance. Please take great care when introducing these lost souls into a new life.

Foraging

You can blame their wild counterparts for all the walking, scratching, and pecking to continually forage for food even though you provide your flock with plenty of good feed and treats. When hens are kept from foraging as their instinct drives them to do, this can create stress and invite behaviors like feather picking. Chickens were not meant to be kept in a cage.

Nesting

Before your hen lays an egg, she will search for an appropriate nesting site. They prefer a darkened space that feels out-of-the-way, but some younger hens have no such protocols and will simply squat in the middle of the hen house to lay their egg on the floor.

When straw or other nesting materials are provided, a hen will spend time arranging her nest to her satisfaction. Your urban hens are lucky that they get to experience the comfort of their nesting boxes. A caged, egg-laying hen has no such luxury, and they must spend their lifetimes being frustrated since they are never able to fluff a nest.

Some hens become close and will often share a nest and even be in it at the same time. If the eggs are fertilized, they may hatch their eggs together and raise their chicks together. Some hens can be unpredictable and may see strange chicks and decide to attack and even kill them.

Broodiness will occur when a hen stops laying and will instead focus on the incubation of eggs already laid. The term most chicken keepers use is to "go broody." This broody hen will sit on a nest and protect it, rarely leaving even to indulge in food or water. A broody hen will task herself with maintaining a constant temperature of the eggs in the nest as well as turning them regularly as part of incubation. An owner may stimulate broodiness in their hens by placing artificial eggs in the nest. If they want to discourage the behavior, they may place the hen in an elevated cage with only an open wire floor. Some breeds have more of an inclination to be broody, and these are the Cochin, Cornish, and the Silkie. They make excellent mothers for chicken eggs but also care for other species like quail, pheasants, geese, or turkeys. Owners have told us that their chicken eggs can also be hatched by using a broody duck, but don't expect them to swim!

Preening

Chickens have a gland near their tail that produces an oil that they use while practicing preening. While preening, a chicken will spread that oil over its feathers, keeping them water-resistant and supple. During a molt (when chickens lose their feathers in favor of new fresh plumage), preening may be an indication of feather follicles that are irritated.

Chicken Chat

If you have never been exposed to chickens and the way they communicate, then you probably weren't aware that they make 30 different sounds with 30 different meanings. As a first-time chicken owner, you may not be able to distinguish a cluck from a chirp, but once you begin to pay attention, you will start to understand chicken speak.

Chick Chat

Did you know that chicks start communicating before they hatch? If the momma hen is around, there will be a conversation between them. After they are born, you may hear some of these sounds.

- Chicks will give off a pleasure thrill that can often be heard when they are settling down for a nap.

- Distress peeps are usually handed out when the youngster is miserable. For example, they may be hot, cold, or hungry.

- A panic peep will be a loud and insistent peep to draw attention to the chick and may be interpreted as a cry for help.

- A fear trill is a loud, sharp, and repeated sound that, above all, relays the message to not harm the frightened chick.

- The startled peep is a sharp chirp.

Momma Says

Hens typically are not very vocal, so when they say something, it's pretty darn important.

- A short cluck that is low-pitched and gets repeated is telling her chicks to stay close.

- The food trumpet is high-pitched and has a staccato sound that sounds like tuck-tuck-tuck. A hen will tell her chicks to get a move on because she just found some food.

- If your hen gives her chicks a hush sound that resembles a vibrating *errrr*, she is telling them to stay put because there is danger.

Hen Speak

While hens aren't very vocal, the girls do tend to announce when they have laid an egg or feel broody.

- The laying cackle announces that your hen has just laid an egg, and she is darn proud of it too.

- A broody hiss may make you believe that you are raising snakes instead of chickens. Your hen will probably fluff their feathers and deliver a dirty look to boot. Broody hens usually do not want you to touch their eggs, and they will probably give you a peck or two as well. You can usually use something to create a barrier between them and you, so that you don't end up with a bunch of holes in your hand.

- On the other hand, a broody growl is much more intimidating than the hiss. This is a warning to leave your hen and her eggs alone, or she will end you.

- Have you ever heard a chicken sing? Well, they don't really sing, but what they do is use rapidly repeated notes randomly. You can compare it to someone blindly humming nothing in particular.

- A contented call can be made by either a hen or a rooster, and it sounds a lot like a low-pitched repetitive sound.

- When a hen is in search of a nest, she will use a nesting call when she chooses one.

- The roosting call is a loud and low-pitched sound that is repeated while the hens settle in for the night.

Rooster Rap

Roosters rule the roost, and they serve their hens by protecting them.

- Crowing. We are all aware that this means that they are in charge.

- The announcement for the arrival of food resembles an excited *tuck-tuck-tuck* sound.

- When a rooster makes a low rumbly sound, this is considered a courtship croon for one of his hens.

- A flying object alert is announced by a chirping sound while your rooster looks toward the sky.

- Roosters can be startled, and they will give a short, intense, and loud squawk.

- Quick repetitive calls tell the flock that there is something dangerous in the vicinity.

- When a rooster or dominant hen sounds an alarm cackle, it sounds like a *kuh-kuh-kuh-kuh-kack*. It is the chicken version of "danger, Will Robinson!"

- A rooster will make a loud warning sound letting his hens know that there is a raptor in the sky.

- The startled squawk can be expressed by a chicken just pecked by another, or it could be that they are slightly injured.

- Distress squawks are loud and repetitive cries by a chicken that has been captured and might be in the process of being carried away. This distress call will garner an attack from the rooster or perhaps another dominant hen.

When you understand how your chickens communicate with one another, you can better understand them and their needs.

Chapter 3:
Know Your Chickens Inside and Out

It's time for the science portion of your lessons on chickens, so don your white lab coat and get ready for some science-fun facts. For instance, the scientific name for a hen is *Gallus gallus domesticus*, and the next time you talk to your friends, you can boast that chickens were first domesticated over 10,000 years ago! Did you know that the top speed of a chicken is six miles per hour? How about their proficiency regarding their flight abilities? Even though chickens have wings, they are known to mostly *fly* only when threatened.

How many breeds of chickens are there? Funny, you should ask. No one knows for sure! According to the American Poultry Association (APA, 2019), they recognize 53 large chicken breeds, which do not include any bantam chicken breeds. If you are into bantam chickens, they have their very own organization, the American Bantam Association, and they maintain their own list of recognized breeds. There are chicken breeds from all over the world that are not part of the APA, so if you are eyeing a breed from Indonesia or Switzerland, they may not be breeds that you can show at exhibitions. Some breeds have been dropped from the APA. For example, a breed called the Russian Orloff was originally recognized by the APA in the year 1875 but then dropped 19 years later. A breed of chicken removed from the APA doesn't mean that it is no longer a breed. It just means that they are no longer considered common.

Chickens were first kept for entertainment in the forms of cockfighting and special ceremonies, depending upon the culture in question. It's an interesting tidbit that chickens were not kept for food until the Hellenistic period (4th-2nd centuries BCE). It is hard to imagine that people before that time didn't realize the true gift that chickens offered to us, especially their yummy eggs! Over the centuries, the chicken's role has changed, and they are now primarily kept for their eggs, meat, and serving as beloved pets.

Chickens in Greek Mythology

In Greek mythology, Alectryon was a young soldier who was ordered to stand guard outside the door of Ares (the god of war) while he was engaged in a love affair with the goddess, Aphrodite.

Poor Alectryon fell asleep while on duty, and the lovers were discovered and reported to Aphrodite's husband. Ares was understandably furious and punished Alectryon by turning him into a rooster. From that time on, Alectryon was never allowed to forget the arrival of the sun each morning and impelled to crow, becoming the god of chickens and roosters for eternity.

Understanding How the Inside of Your Chicken Works

When you understand how the inside of your chicken works, it helps you produce the best eggs, meat, and bloodlines. So here's the scoop from the inside of the coop.

Biology

Fun fact: chickens were the first birds to have their DNA sequenced; this took place in 2004.

Roosters can be easily identified by their long, flowing tail feathers, brighter plumage, comb, or the development of spurs on the males' legs. You may have noticed that males are always the more colorful ones when it comes to separating the male from the female.

Adult chickens will sport a fleshy crest on their heads, which are called combs or cockscomb, and under their beaks are hanging flaps of skin which are referred to as wattles. Both male and female chickens will have wattles and combs, but overall, they are far more pronounced in the roosters.

Domesticated chickens, while possessing the ability to fly, are not able to do so for long distances. The typical chicken can fly for short distances like over fences or into trees to roost from predators. They may occasionally fly to flee danger.

According to the *Guinness Book of World Records* (2021), the oldest chicken died at the ripe old age of 16 due to heart failure. The average lifespan of a chicken, depending upon the breed, is five to 10 years.

Did you know that chickens dream? According to Andy Schneider (2017), they do, and they even experience REM sleep. So, what do you think your chickens dream about? Raising their chicks? Tasty mealworms? Maybe just enjoying a good swing!

Anatomy

According to Veronica Hirsch (2003), chickens can see in color, possess a small brain, and possess a large hypothalamus, which is responsible for the autonomic nervous system. Their well-developed hypothalamus controls their body temperature, thirst, hunger, sleep, and any emotional activity your chickens may experience.

Overall, chickens have a lightweight skeleton, and some of their pneumatic bones (connected to the respiratory system) are even hollow. Unlike humans, a chicken possesses rather rigid lungs that do not expand or contract in conjunction with the chicken breathing, and they are attached to the chicken's ribs. Therefore, when holding a chicken, you must be careful not to restrict the movement of the breastbone because this must be allowed to move freely, or you may risk suffocating your bird.

Chickens have no teeth and use their beaks to shred their food. Their barbed tongue then moves the food back toward the esophagus. Within the esophagus is a small pouch called a crop, where the chicken's system can store the food for a short time before moving it off to the stomach. After that, the food moves from the stomach into the gizzard. Inside this area, the food will be crushed with the help of any gravel and grit that the bird has swallowed before moving into the intestines. Here is where proteins and enzymes (supplied by the gut, pancreas, and liver) will dissolve the food and remove all the nutrients. After the intestines, the food paste will move into the ceca. It is here that chicken poop comes from.

From eating to pooping, the chicken will take about four hours to process the food, eight hours if they are laying, and 12 hours if the hen is broody. If you guessed that the poop of a broody hen would smell worse, you would be correct.

Hens are born with two ovaries, but usually, only one of them will develop and be functional. Typically, it's the left one. When hens lay eggs, they will pass through the cloaca, a chamber that is also the route her feces take via the rectum. For this reason, the outside of an egg may be contaminated by bacteria, germs, and other potential diseases that may, on occasion, pass through the shell and into the egg itself.

This is why commercial poultry flocks are often held to strict guidelines for disinfection and are often subject to vigorous inspection procedures.

The composition of a chicken's bones is mainly calcium and phosphorus and can be split into two different types.

- Medullary: The bone marrow within the center of these bones makes blood cells and allows the storage of calcium. Bones of this type are found in the legs, shoulder blades, and ribs.

- Pneumatic bones are the hollow ones We mentioned before and are connected via air sacs to the respiratory system. Examples of these bones are the pelvis, collar bones, skull, and humerus (arm bone).

While watching your birds at play, you have probably noticed that the neck and backbone look very flexible. Well, you are correct! Their spine contains 39 bones, and between this and their neck being quite long, this can provide a bird with a large range of motion while looking for food. For example, chickens can turn their heads 180 degrees!

The largest bone found in a chicken's body is the sternum. This bone covers half of your chicken's body cavity, and even their wings are attached to the sternum by strong muscles.

A chicken's legs are similar to human anatomy until you get to the hip bone, which is fused with a chicken's backbone.

Reproduction

First-time chicken owners may not be aware of this, but it is really important to those potential owners in urban areas that do not allow roosters; you do not need a rooster to get eggs! That's right; a hen is born with a predetermined number of eggs. There are only two reasons that you need a rooster. The first one is if you want their protection for your girls, and the second is if you want baby chicks.

Roosters may *dance* in a circle near a hen to begin a courting ritual. He may lower his wing closest to the hen in question. If his dance triggers a hen to respond, the rooster may mount the hen and proceed with mating.

When a rooster and hen mate, the hen can maintain the sperm in her oviducts or expel the sperm. Should the hen keep the sperm, it will be viable for fertilizing her eggs for about 30 days. This kept sperm will fertilize the eggs, and the hen will lay fertilized eggs. If you see her become broody, you will notice her tuck several eggs into a nest, and she will sit on them until they hatch.

Eggs are a wonder of nature because they contain all the nutrition a young chick needs to grow. Eggs are usually laid in a grouping because nature realizes that some will hatch and survive, but some won't. Chicken offspring are better developed at the time of their hatching because they will be able to walk and stand. Other baby birds are sequestered in their nests until they develop enough to fly, hop, or stand.

Health & Wellness

Everyone likes to start with healthy stock and keep them that way, but if one of your flock isn't feeling well, it will not be difficult to ascertain that something is wrong. A healthy bird will be active, vibrant, and perky. Their feathers will be glossy, and their eyes will look bright. Should one of your chickens act uncharacteristically lifeless, there will be some tell-tale signs you might notice. For example, their eyes may look dull, and their feathers could appear dull and ruffled. If something is wrong, you may hear noisy, labored breathing.

People with backyard chickens never want any of their flock members to experience illness because our hens become like any other family pet. Because chickens cost so little to purchase or maintain, it seems unfair that most of their diseases are often difficult to diagnose and costly to treat. Smaller, urban flocks are more unlikely to see chicken diseases, unlike the large commercial operations, but you should be aware of them.

There are four main disease types you should be aware of:

- Behavioral diseases may show up as pecking at other birds, excessively plucking of feathers, or acting aggressively. Birds suffering from stress may revert to cannibalism and begin eating eggs. Because chickens can start this habit, we do not agree with giving them crushed eggshells. Keep your chickens comfortable and make sure they have fantastic nutrition to help curb the development of behavioral disorders.

- Metabolic or nutritional diseases are caused by unhealthy living environments. Your chickens can experience a reduction in eggs, develop soft bones, soft beaks, or even exhibit lameness due to poor nutrition and exercise. Taking proper care of your birds will prevent most of these issues.

- Infectious diseases can be born from bacterial, viral, or fungal issues and will be spread easily from bird to bird. You can protect your flock by isolating any birds exhibiting symptoms that aren't normal.

- Parasitic diseases are often brought about by contact with other infected birds or because of compromised living conditions. Common culprits include ticks, mites, lice, fleas, or roundworms, and they will often be visible but cause your birds to have feather damage, irritation, or parasites in your birds' feces. Keep any chicken housing clean to help prevent parasitic poultry diseases.

Aspergillosis

This respiratory disease is caused by a fungal species known as aspergillus, but many refer to it as brooder's pneumonia or fungal pneumonia. This is common to bird species but is non-contagious. Younger stock will be the most susceptible to this type of infection, although if you have older birds that have been under a lot of stress or have had bouts of poor health, they can also develop chronic aspergillosis.

One of the most common sources of aspergillosis is from contaminated poultry bedding with high levels of ammonia. Still, it can also be present in inhaled spores, or a contaminated hatching machine, or during incubation of infected eggs. This type of respiratory infection can be either acute or chronic. Poor quality of feed can also be a cause of this respiratory disease.

- Acute infections usually target younger chickens with symptoms that develop within the first three to five days after the initial exposure. What you might witness is rapid, open-mouthed breathing caused by gradual air passage obstruction. When the disease progresses, you will notice a lack of appetite, increased thirst, drowsiness, emaciation, eye swelling, blindness, and torticollis, which is a twisting of their neck to one side.

- Chronic aspergillosis will typically affect an older chicken with a compromised immune system. Chronic cases can lead to severe neurological dysfunction, respiratory distress, blindness, and eye discharge.

Unfortunately, there is no known treatment for aspergillosis, so the best prevention is to keep your chicken's habitat clean and ensure that you are feeding them with quality ingredients. Here is your prevention checklist:

- Keep the chicken coop clean and free from bedding contamination.

- Clean and sanitize any equipment used in your hatchery and brooding areas.

- Keep your grain and water feeders clean to avoid any contamination.

- Store your chicken's feed in clean, dry containers. Always throw away any spilled and uneaten food to prevent fungal growth.

- Replace nesting boxes and bedding regularly to impede the growth of fungus. Discard any wet bedding because even if it's only water, it will break down shavings or other beddings to create an environment for fungal growth.

- Keep any eggs that will be hatched away from dusty areas that may have spores.

Coccidiosis

Your bird may be immune to one kind of coccidiosis, but there are still five other species of this parasite. This is probably more commonly experienced by the small flock keeper, and you will notice that your chicken has loose droppings, weight loss, or bloody or watery diarrhea. Coccidiosis is caused by a parasite damaging your chicken's gut wall. The parasites enter your chicken's system by ingesting them, whether found in contaminated water, soil, or even feces from other infected birds.

Coccidiosis most often occurs during spring and summer because this is when the soil is warm and moist, providing ideal conditions for parasites. Your younger stock will be more susceptible than your older flock members. Once a bird has been infected and cured, it should never contract that same strain of coccidiosis. Most affected are chicks, which is why it's a good idea to start them off on a medicated starter feed which is formulated specifically to boost the immune system and protect against parasites.

This can be treated with antibiotics or with sulmet, which is added to their drinking water. There are several medications and treatments, and many of them can be found at your local farm store. And great news, treatments always work quickly! Treatment will usually run for seven days, but your sick chickens may often show improvement in 24 hours.

Egg Bound

The term "egg bound" is used for hens that have difficulties passing an egg. Depending upon the hen, it could just be a single occurrence. However, some hens can develop a chronic problem. Either way, this can be a critical situation for your hen.

When a hen is egg-bound, they tend to stand upright, like a penguin, and their abdomens will feel hot. In the best-case scenario, the egg may pass, however, should the egg get caught in the hen, it can result in her death. If an egg breaks inside of your hen, she will die.

You can help your hen by immersing her vent and backside in a tub of warm water and then gently massaging the area around the egg, but you must be careful not to break the egg. Another option would be to place a small amount of mineral oil on a latex glove and gently massage the oil up the chicken's vent.

You should never breed a chronic egg-bound hen as this can be passed on to the next generation.

Fowl Pox

Fowl pox can show up as either a dry or wet form. If you are experiencing the wet form, the disease will show up as lesions that appear around the mouth, and your bird may show discharge from their eyes. The dry form will look like wart-like lesions that show up in the unfeathered area of your bird. These lesions should heal in about two weeks.

Generally, sick chickens should be quarantined and made as comfortable as possible. There is no specific treatment for fowl pox, but it should go away after a few weeks. Mosquitoes can transmit this disease from flock to flock.

Infectious Bronchitis

Yes, chickens can catch a cold! What's more, is that it is just as contagious as the human equivalent. Should your flock experience a cold outbreak, you will notice a drop in egg production, their appetite will decline, and there may be a discharge from either the birds' eyes or nostrils, perhaps both, and your birds will exhibit labored breathing.

Similar to humans, they pretty much have to ride out their colds. Not much can be done except to give your birds some antibiotics for a few days. At least we can curl up in bed and drink chicken noodle soup.

Though there are some preventative vaccines out there, they come with no guarantee. Your best defense is to practice biosecurity and keep rodents to a minimum.

Marek's Disease

When you order chicks from a hatchery, you are probably going to hear about Marek's Disease, commonly referred to as MD, but also known as fowl paralysis.

MD is considered avian cancer that is very contagious and transmitted via the air found inside a poultry house. This disease affects mostly young birds, and unvaccinated chicks between 10 to 12 weeks old can show up to a 50% mortality rate.

Symptoms include paralysis of the legs or wings, tumors on feather follicles, depression, diarrhea, and a general sense of being weak. You may also see combs that shrivel or blindness that often occurs in only one eye.

Some hatcheries make it a practice to vaccinate all their chicks for MD, while others may charge a fee for vaccinating your chicks. Even though you are unlikely to experience MD within your flock because of high vaccination rates, there is no known cure or treatment for this disease. Since it is a virus, it will be transmitted from bird to bird, and any that experience this disease will be a carrier for life, so you will have to remove it from the rest of your flock as soon as possible and keep it separate.

If you are hatching chicks, they should be vaccinated upon emerging from their shells. You should know that the smallest dose available is for 200 chicks and that any unused portion of the vaccine cannot be saved for later. Anything left over must be discarded.

Newcastle Disease

This is a respiratory disease that affects your chicken's ability to breathe and creates nasal discharge, murky-looking eyes, and as with most diseases, a reduction in egg production. Sometimes, though not as common, birds can experience a twisting in their neck and paralysis that takes over their legs and wings. There are varying strains that may appear to be more lethal than others.

While your adult chickens should recover from Newcastle disease and will not be carriers, your chicks will most likely not survive. You can give your affected birds antibiotics for a few days to avoid any additional infections while your chicken is recovering.

This disease is typically carried by wild birds, so keeping your chickens vaccinated is key, along with practicing good sanitation in and around your chicken's living quarters. You should also know that you can infect your birds if the disease is carried on your clothing or shoes.

Pullorum

This is a nonrespiratory bacterial disease. In most states within the US, this is a reportable disease. What this means is if one chicken has pullorum, then the entire flock must be destroyed, whether they are ill or not. While this disease is not a threat to humans, it could wipe out the poultry industry if allowed to get out of hand. Fortunately, it is extremely rare in North America.

The usual way this is spread is from hen to chick, through the egg, although there is also a danger of it being transmitted by contaminated incubators, houses, or equipment. When present in chicks, it may start with excessive huddling, droopiness, gasping, a pasted vent, and excretions that appear to be chalk-white stained with green bile. This is a serious illness that, if suspected, should be verified by your veterinarian. Any outbreak is handled by your local state or federal regulatory agency.

Wry Neck

Other common names for this condition include stargazing, twisted neck, or crookneck, and this usually affects newborn chicks, and on occasion, full-grown chickens. Tell-tale signs of this condition include difficulty to stand, and your chicken's neck will twist often, looking like it is stuck looking upward toward the stars.

Wry neck is usually the result of a genetic disorder, a head injury, a vitamin deficiency, or by the ingestion of certain toxins. Chickens can live with this condition; however, they may be highly stressed because eating and drinking will be frustrating and difficult. In addition, they will be unable to move very well and may get picked on by the rest of the flock.

Separating affected birds is the kindest thing you can do for them because this will keep their stress levels down. While separated, you can raise the affected bird's vitamin intake by targeting the addition of vitamin E and selenium. These should be given to your affected bird two or three times each day until you see any improvement in your chicken's condition. Natural sources of vitamin E include spinach, broccoli, dandelion greens, and asparagus.

You will have to be patient because wry neck does not go away quickly. It can take upwards of a month before the condition resolves itself, and you would be wise to continue the extra vitamin intake for at least two weeks after that, making sure that your chicken is back to its old self.

The best prevention is to feed a high-quality diet to your flock. And there certainly isn't anything wrong with adding in some goodies that provide vitamin E as a bonus treat!

Poultry Pests

Let's face it; nobody likes pests. However, if you allow wet litter to remain in your coop, you will have your fair share of the little creepy-crawlies. This is one of the main reasons we are so finicky about cleanliness. We just hate bugs!

The House Fly

Poultry poop is the preferred place for these pests to breed, and since flies are known to carry several diseases, you are going to want to keep your chicken manure pile far from your coop.

Blow Flies

These pests love to breed in broken eggs and wet garbage. Daily cleanup is essential to prevent a build-up of these pests.

Lice

On the bright side, poultry lice are host-specific, so their lice will not transfer to you or the family dog. Chickens will contract lice from wild birds or other chickens. As we mentioned previously, your chicken's dust baths will help out with parasites.

Mites

While several different mites can affect poultry, the two most popular are the scaly leg mites and depluming mites.

Scaly leg mites are described as being round, tiny, and flat. These mites will burrow under the scales of your chicken's feet and lower legs, raising those scales and giving your chicken the appearance of having deformed feet. You can either rub in petroleum jelly or dip their legs in linseed oil and then wipe the legs clean. Whatever treatment you choose, you should apply it for several weeks at the rate of once or twice a week.

Depluming mites can be found on your chicken's skin at the base of their feather shafts. Depluming mites are so named because your chicken will peck at the mites and will even pull out their own feathers, leading to bacterial skin infections and even cannibalism. Permethrin spray and dust treatments are the most commonly used for these mites.

It seems that most chicken maladies can be easily curbed by limiting exposure to wild birds, keeping your coop clean, and feeding a good quality diet. Let your chickens be happy, keep them stress-free, allow them to enjoy their dust baths and should any of your chickens not seem to be themselves, keep them isolated.

Keep a Wellness Checklist

Routine health checks can head off any minor problems before they progress. If you have a flock of fewer than ten birds, you may not feel the need to keep a written record, but it can be a handy thing to refer to. If you are breeding and hatching chicks, this may be a more important step.

You can set up a basic health chart in any application like Excel. Just remember to check all vital areas and leave room to make some notes. You can perform this monthly unless you have some chickens that seem under the weather, in which case you may want to adjust your chart for daily observations during their illness. This is our basic chart, but you can change it in any way that suits you.

Name / Breed	Comb /Wats	Beak	Eyes	Feathers	Crop	Legs & Feet	Vent	Active	Remarks
Hera/ BO	✓	✓	✓	✓	✓	✓	✓	✓	molting
Bertha/ BR	✓	✓	✓	✓	✓	✓	✓	✓	dusted 4 mites
Rosie / RIR	✓	✓	✓	✓	✓	✓	✓	✓	broody

1. The first column is for your chicken's name, breed, or even tag number.

2. The second column is only for the comb and wattles and how they look. If your hen has been molting or brooding, this may influence how the comb looks. If you see any indication of an injury, it may need to be addressed. If you are in a colder climate, you may want to check these areas for frostbite.

3. The third column covers the appearance of your chicken's beak. You should check how they are aligning or if, by some odd occurrence, it may be fractured. If you suspect that it is overgrown at the tip and your chicken is experiencing

problems eating and drinking, you can file the tip with a Dremel tool. But whatever you do, don't get carried away because their beaks are sensitive.

4. The fourth column is all about your chicken's eyes and whether they appear to be bright and alert. Make notations about any drainage or discharge you might see. If you have concerns, a veterinarian can take a swab of the discharge and have it tested. *Tip: Should you have a sight-challenged bird, always keep your feeders and waterers in the same place.*

5. The fifth column is all about feathers and their appearance. Your chicken's feathers should appear to be glossy and tight unless you have a specialty breed like a Frizzle or a Frizzle-cross. *Tip: Within your flock, the best layers are the quickest to molt and regrow their feathers. This is a perfect time to put a star by their names, so you have identified your egg superstars!*

6. The sixth column is where your chicken will store their food while it is waiting to be digested. The rule of thumb is that it should be empty in the morning and full at bedtime. Crops should never feel rock-hard, only mushy. If your hen's crop feels hard, it could mean that she has an impaction. If so, you will need to get her to the vet ASAP. Signs of a sour crop include breath

that smells like rancid milk, an unwillingness to eat, or acting lethargic.

7. The seventh column is for observations about the chicken's legs and feet. Scales on the feet should be smooth and uniform and should never appear to be raised or uneven. If you have a chicken with feathers on its toes, you will need to check this carefully since it can be very easy to overlook something due to the heavy feathering.

8. The eighth column covers the vent, and any chicken that is laying will have a pink, moist appearance. Should a chicken be past its prime in laying, its vent will appear to be pale and dry even if they are laying the occasional egg here and there. If you have a hen that has a prolapsed vent, she must be isolated from her flockmates for her safety as the others may peck at it. During this time of inspection, you should trim off any poop-filled feathers.

9. The ninth column is very simply covering if your chicken is displaying normal activity.

10. At the end of your line is a final column for any general remarks you may wish to make. This can cover anything from molting to the removal of bumblefoot.

Choosing the Best Chicken Breed for You

Almost any chicken will make a fantastic addition to your family, but some breeds are more friendly, easier to handle, and are generally calmer than other breeds. Of course, how you raise and treat your chickens has a lot to do with how friendly they are and how they interact with others. There are far too many breeds of chickens to list them all, but We have pulled out our favorites when it comes to new chicken owners. When chicks are tiny balls of fluff, it is hard to be objective about their breeds because all chicks are adorable, but if you consider one from our list below, you won't be disappointed.

Araucanas

This breed of chicken will lay beautiful blue or green eggs and weather the cold well. The hens are friendly, but the roosters can be more aggressive. There are a couple of characteristics that separate the Araucanas from other chickens. They possess tufts, which are found around their ear lobes or neck area, and they have no tail! Yes, that's right, they have no tail nor tail bone. They also have no wattles, a pea comb, and have facial feathers. Araucanas do well in areas of confinement, but they do enjoy fresh grass. This breed makes a great mother, though they do tend to be a broody chicken and just a little bit on the flighty side, and as far as their ranking within the pecking order, they tend to be in the middle of the flock. It is always fun to have colorful eggs to collect, and the Araucana is known to produce three to four medium-sized eggs each week. This breed lives around seven to eight years and is a relatively healthy breed. The roosters for this breed are known to be cranky but not aggressive. It should be noted that this breed can struggle when it comes to hot environments and humid weather.

Australorp

They will give you big, brown-colored eggs and are surprisingly consistent egg layers. This breed of chicken was originally developed from Orpington stock, and they tend to thrive in colder climates. Their feathers feel soft, and their large size is a delight to see in your backyard flock (although there is also a bantam-sized version of this chicken). The Australorp is considered to be one of the best multipurpose chickens that you can add to your flock, and their friendliness makes them a perfect pet. While the hens are very friendly, it should be noted that the roosters can be aggressive toward children or in general.

Barred Plymouth Rock

The Barred Rock chicken is the standard hen that everyone pictures when you start to talk about chickens. Besides being a classic breed, these hens are calm as well as productive. The Barred Rock is a favorite of backyard flock owners for over 100 years because they are hardy, docile, and productive. This breed is known for its barred black and white feathers, and once they get to know you, they will prove how friendly they are by begging for treats. This breed will also make excellent therapy birds because they enjoy being picked up and cuddled! These hens settle well into the backyard coop and love to forage for food. She will lay light brown medium to large eggs to the tune of around four each week, which averages out to be about 200 a year. Hens are not overly broody birds but make good mothers. This breed has no major health concerns and tolerates confinement, but they love to free-range. Although the roosters are protective of their girls, they have been known to sit on the eggs so the hen can have a break, and although they tend to be more laid back than many other breeds of roosters, they should still not be left alone with small children.

Buff Orpington

If a plump hen comes to mind when you picture a chicken, then you are probably dreaming of a Buff Orpington. Considering how popular these chickens are with backyard chicken enthusiasts, it is hard to imagine that these chickens were considered endangered until 2016, according to the Happy Chicken Coop (2021). Orpingtons are available in both large and bantam sizes, with the large hen weighing in at about eight pounds. Generally, all the Orpingtons are described as being docile, but the buff tends to be calm, friendly, and addicted to being cuddled. As long as they are kept dry, they will tolerate cold well, but in warmer climates, they will need and seek out shade to hide in during the heat of the day. Hens can be broody and also be great mothers, often accepting and hatching other eggs placed under them. Even though the hens are thought to be great for families with children, you should know that they have strong beaks that can peck pretty hard! Because they are friendly and docile birds, they are often an excellent choice for a 4-H animal. Their ability to tolerate a lot of handling, strange environments, and confinement, makes them a great show bird as well because it seems that it is tough to ruffle their feathers. They are good egg producers and lay about 200 to 280 large brown eggs each year. Since this is such a docile chicken, you should avoid putting them in a flock with more aggressive breeds such as Rhode Island Reds or Welsummers because they will get picked on, and they are most likely at the bottom of any flock's pecking order. Due to their dense feathering, you should check them frequently for any signs of lice and mites. Healthwise, one thing you should monitor is their weight since they tend to be lazy and obese. A Buff Orpington hen will, without a doubt, be one of your favorite hens.

Cochin Bantams

These are also a great choice if you have children, and the cochins do have a full-sized equivalent. These bantam-sized chickens tend to work well when dealing with autistic children because of their friendly temperament and the fact that they love to be held or even sit next to a child on a swing. While the full-sized roosters rarely become aggressive, the bantam size roosters are not as mellow and can be fairly aggressive. Described as head-to-toe feathers, once you see one of these, they will stick in your mind, especially since you cannot see most of their toes, only the feathers that cover them. Cochins are slow to mature and can take up to two years to be fully grown. This particular breed tolerates small spaces, so if you don't have a lot of room, this particular breed might be an excellent alternative. It should also be noted that Cochins are prone to become obese, and they do not forage for much, preferring instead to park in front of your feeders. For these larger and often overweight birds, you should provide some roosts near the ground so that they do not injure themselves by jumping down. Because they are *puffy*, you will need to check them regularly for lice and mites. If you choose to keep the cochin, either large or small, you should be aware that you will need to keep them in a safe space since they are easily picked off by predators. They get along well with other chickens and sport cool feathers on their feet. Both roosters and hens tend to love people and, like the Mille Fleurs, have winning personalities. These chickens are not the best layers, but they make up for it with their tolerance and love for children.

Easter Egger

Even though this is not considered a pure breed, they are great with children and also offer a bantam-sized chicken. You should think of them as the lovable mutts of the chicken world. There is nothing wrong with Easter Eggers, but you should know the difference, and since they are a hybrid of either the Ameraucana or the Araucana, they may end up with the muffs or beards known to be a characteristic of these breeds. There are no strict breed standards, but Easter Eggers will often lay a wide variety of egg colors, and they possess outstanding personalities. These chickens have become a backyard favorite because they are friendly, low-maintenance, and deliver some show-stopping egg colors. Make sure that you give serious consideration to adding one or more of these curious and gentle birds to your flock.

Frizzles

Will always bring a smile to your children's faces (and probably yours too)! These birds look just like their name implies because they lack conventional feathers and instead sport ones that turn up instead of lying flat. This lends them a messy-looking appearance that is endearing. You can also get variances within chicken breeds, so you could even see frizzled Cochins, frizzled Orpingtons, and yes, sometimes even frizzled Silkies. Between their fun, wind-blown look and the fact that they don't mind the activity levels of children, the

Frizzles make great chickens for your children. Oddly enough, how you breed a Frizzle is to cross a Frizzled parent with a traditionally feathered chicken. If you try to breed a Frizzle rooster and hen, there is a 25 percent chance that they will have brittle feathers (which could prove to be life-threatening). These are very patient chickens, but this can also make them a target for hens with a bullying nature. As with your bantams on this list, you should have plenty of feeding stations, so your favorite chickens never miss a meal.

Jersey Giant

Aptly named, the Jersey Giant is the largest purebred chicken in the US and likely the world! The size of this bird is impressive, and luckily, they are gentle giants! This breed of chicken was created around 1917 in New Jersey, and by 2001 the breed was listed as being critically endangered. There is still some work to do in order to keep this breed safe because, in 2017, this chicken was still listed on the watch list, but backyard breeders are embracing this breed and helping it make a comeback. Roosters can weigh as much as 13 to 15 pounds, with the hens weighing around 11 pounds. Both hens and roosters are friendly, docile, and mellow birds, and despite their size, they are generally good with children, although their stature might be found to be intimidating. The hens will not go broody much, and unfortunately, because of their weight, they are prone to breaking their eggs. In these cases, it may be worth it to set these eggs under a broody but smaller hen.

Overall, the Jersey Giant is a great choice for the backyard flock owner since they get along well with other breeds, and most of the other chickens give them a wide berth simply because of their size. This breed is easier to handle than some breeds and never flighty. Since they are larger birds, hawks also tend to give them a pass. This chicken is one of those instances where you would want to increase your coop size based upon your chickens' needs. While not a top egg producer, they still lay 150 to 200 eggs or an average of two to four eggs each week. It's no surprise that their eggs are on the larger side and range from light to medium brown. Because of their size, they are slow to mature, and considering their size and weight; this is another breed that you would want to provide perches lower to the ground to avoid leg injuries. If you have a smaller free-range area, this may not be enough space to host these giants. These are easy birds to raise, but their feed intake will be more costly because of their slower rate of growth.

Black Copper Marans

While described as a docile bird, the Maran is not at all cuddly. Right now, the hens from this breed are making a comeback in the backyard coop, especially because of the dark, chocolate-colored eggs that it lays. Overall, this breed is described as quiet and gentle, but the roosters have been known to be more aggressive with other roosters. However, they have proven to be hardy in the winter months if given adequate shelter in their coop environment. The average hen production is between 150 to 200 eggs each year or about three per week. This breed is a bit more costly than most, and if you live in a colder climate, their overly large comb may make them more likely for frostbite, which can cause their comb to die off. Overall, hatchery chicks are most likely your best avenue for purchase unless you are looking for a show chicken, in which case, you may want to investigate some reputable breeders.

Mille Fleurs

This Belgian chicken is kid-friendly, and even though they are on the smaller side, their personalities are *huge*. Mille Fleur bantams were originally developed to be show birds, and they normally weigh about two pounds. These birds tend to love to be in the company of humans and would also make a fantastic therapy chicken! This breed of chicken is usually the first at the coop door every morning waiting for their human to arrive. The roosters are known to be as patient as the hens and typically don't show any territorial actions. The only problem you as an owner will have with this gentle-natured bird is that between their size and demeanor, they will always be on the bottom of the flock's pecking order. To make sure that they get their fair share of the chow, you should have plenty of feeding areas so that they don't get pushed out.

Plymouth Rock

Known as one of the oldest breeds in America, the Plymouth Rock breed was at one time the nation's primary source of chicken eggs and meat. This breed is known for its black and white bar plumage. These hens average about four eggs each week, which equals around 200 eggs each year. In the first couple of years, the hens lay well, but by the third year, most owners will see a decline in the number of eggs they receive. However, this seems to balance out since these hens are known to lay into their tenth year. These hens usually make good sitters and even better moms. The Barred Rocks are generally mellow birds that are known for good attitudes and getting along well with all their coop companions. Even the roosters in this breed are described as docile, calm, and sweet. They are often described as curious birds that love to follow their owners around just in case they are hiding some treats. Even though they tolerate confinement, they relish their free space. This breed has considerable longevity and can live from 10 to 12 years. They are a good choice for first-time chicken owners, and if you like to make a fuss over your chickens, this breed is a fantastic choice, and should your children be involved in 4-H, this would be an excellent breed for them to exhibit. This is a versatile breed that can fill any direction you wish to take.

Rhode Island Reds

This is an appropriate choice for someone who has never had chickens before. They are friendly, easy-going, and easy to care for. Someone new to chickens will be pleased with their egg production (250 to 300 light brown eggs a year). This popular breed is found in every corner of the globe, and they are personable as well as hardy. Since they are active foragers, they are entertaining to observe and usually end up somewhere in the middle of the pack in the pecking order. While the Reds tolerate confinement, they do enjoy getting out and stretching their legs and certainly aren't opposed to the occasional mouse that crosses its path! The hens are laid back for adults and children, but the roosters can be aggressive. If you are hemming and hawing about what chickens to add to your flock, choose some red hens because you just cannot go wrong with this choice. The only problem you might find with the Rhode Island Reds is that you may not find all their eggs because they are predator savvy and like to hide them.

Silkies

Silkies are great with children, and as their name implies, they will feel, well, silky! A Silky's feathers are different because they lack barbicels, which is what gives other feathers their stiff appearance. Silkies are known to be quiet and tolerant as well as good mothers. They are known for becoming broody and will even hatch other breeds of chickens.

Sussex

This breed has been around for a couple of centuries, and with good reason, the Sussex is a dual-purpose hen that provides steady egg production as well as being a good meat bird. The gentle disposition of this bird makes them a favorite because they are easy to handle. The Sussex is considered a year-round bird that is hardy in the winter and will tolerate the hot rays of summer as long as there are shady places and cool water. Both the hens and roosters are described as being mellow, and since they are not an aggressive breed, they should never be put in with breeds that demonstrate any signs of violent behavior. The Sussex will always be at the bottom of the flock's pecking order and may even be subjected to flock bullying. This breed is an excellent choice for first-time chicken owners since they are low maintenance, fast to mature, and docile. Their eggs are brown and tend to run largely with about four to five eggs each week, translating to 208 to 260 eggs each year. One interesting thing about this breed is that they will continue to lay during the winter months when other breeds are on strike. They tend to be broody and make great mothers. Except for leaning toward obesity, this breed of chicken has no health issues that stand out. If you want their egg production to remain steady, you will have to make sure they stay slim and trim. Children love this breed since these birds enjoy the company of humans and like being held and stroked. If you talk to them, you may just receive some chicken conversation when they decide to chime in. Besides being an excellent breed for beginner owners, they also make great birds for 4-H projects.

White Leghorn

While white is the color most closely associated with the Leghorn, they do come in other colors. Leghorns are intelligent, active, and resourceful birds that are also a bit on the aloof and flighty side. They can also be described as noisy birds, so they are not for people that have nearby neighbors who can get easily annoyed. The Leghorn hens are popular because they will lay 280 to 320 eggs each year or four or more eggs per week. An odd fact about this breed of hen is that her eggs start off as large and are actually transformed into extra-large by the end of her laying cycle. They have been purposely bred to resist being broody, and they are considered to be pretty poor mothers, so if you want to raise chicks, you will either have to get a surrogate Silkie to sit on her eggs or place them in an incubator. If they are in colder climates, you may have to watch for frostbitten combs and wattles, treating them with Vaseline. Leghorns are not noted to be overly friendly or cuddly, and if you cannot locate them, you may find them roosting in a nearby tree. They can still provide you with hours of chicken entertainment, so pull up a chair and watch for a while.

And Now for Something Completely Different... Guineas!

While not quite a chicken, Guinea hens are an occasional layer, but their best job is as a pest control agent. They can be a bit difficult to allow free range without barriers as Guineas tend to go *walkabout* to borrow an Australian phrase. Visitors will definitely give these birds a second glance because they just cannot figure out where to place them. Is it a turkey? A chicken? While they are chicken-like birds, this family of fowl will scour your gardens, pastures, and yards for beetles, locusts, spiders, ticks, cockroaches, wasps, flies, termites, grubs, snails, and even scorpions!

Guineas are native to Africa but arrived in North America with early settlers. They are a rather unique-looking bird with its white featherless face, gray polka-dot feathers, and bright red wattles. Because these birds prefer weeds, seeds, and insects (along with the occasional mouse or scorpion), they are often put to work clearing rows between crops and hunting the pests that reside in the fields.

Free-ranging guineas will spend almost all of their day foraging, and if you have several, they work in tandem and snap up anything they startle, for example, a small snake. They are a bit noisier than chickens because when they find some prey, the pack of them will all emit whistles, clicks, and chirps of excitement and commentary on their subject. If you have less than forgiving neighbors, guineas may not be a good fit for your flock because they are noisy. Be forewarned that they can easily destroy blossoming plants in a heartbeat. However, they can provide some great protection for the rest of your flock.

Guineas do not take confinement very well, so they may also not be a good fit if you have limited space. While guineas are not overly friendly, dislike snow, and are difficult to catch, they are considered low-maintenance poultry that will lay about 100 eggs each year. Guineas that are raised with chickens are tamer than guineas that are the sole species of bird. While you may find that a guinea will mate with a chicken, the sterile offspring tend to look a little like a vulture.

Since guineas are not known to be the best mothers, many keetlings are hatched using an incubator. A keet or keetling is what a baby guinea is called, and if you want to raise a few guineas and plan to free-range, we suggest that you start with keets as opposed to purchasing full-grown birds. While still babies, the keets become accustomed to their new home and will be less likely to split the first chance they get, unlike adult guineas.

Because keets are extra small and extremely delicate, they are fragile and can be trampled during their first few weeks of life. Until they reach the three weeks of age mark, keets should be kept off to themselves and before being moved into larger coop areas. You will not see any feathers develop on them until they are about a month old, and these will be a camouflage-brown color. They are not ready to care for themselves until their gray feathers have grown in.

To feed keets, you should try a 21 to 23 percent protein feed, like a commercial turkey starter or even mashed-up hard-boiled eggs mixed with a little cornmeal, oatmeal, or cottage cheese. When they reach four weeks of age, you can switch them to an 18% grower ration.

Now for the tarantula story that we promised you earlier! Once upon a time, we were visiting some friends out in Arizona who kept a substantial amount of guinea fowl. Suddenly, there was quite a ruckus from the yard, and our friend encouraged us to watch a tarantula migration that had drifted right through the guinea pen area. It was a massacre! Guineas were snapping up those spiders faster than you could blink, and for years afterward, during other tarantula migrations, the herd traveled out and around the guinea enclosure! We are positive that the hens were very disappointed.

Chapter 4:
Know What You Are Getting Into

Raising your own chickens can be a great experience, that is, as long as you have taken the time to prepare for ownership and reviewed all the essential needs that you and your chickens will need in order for you to both be happy.

The last thing that anyone wants to do is jump into a hobby farm without knowing what to expect. This can lead to becoming overwhelmed and frustrated, making chicken ownership a less than fantastic experience.

First and foremost, you need to check any restrictions regarding the keeping of chickens on your property. There are usually rules that prevent you from owning a rooster. Still, they may stipulate how many chickens you are allowed, how far your chicken coop and run must be from a neighboring property line, or even if there is a fine involved in chicken ownership. One of our good friends was disturbed to find out that her city would fine her fifty dollars per bird each day for the breaking of any city rules governing the ownership of chickens.

Can You Do Chicken Math?

If you have space, always plan for more chickens eventually. However, there is this freak of nature called *chicken math*. How this works is that you have plans for one to three chickens, but it quickly turns into three to five, and suddenly you have about ten hens.

The point is that chickens are super addictive, and when you see some cute chicks, then you will want to add more to your flock. Chickens are as addictive as potato chips, and the bottom line is you're going to need a bigger coop!

Be Prepared

Chickens, like any other pet or farm animal, are a daily commitment. It's not that they are complicated because once you have their care down to a routine, you will find that caring for your flock is very easy. Even novice owners will be able to break down which chores are daily, weekly, monthly, or even yearly. It goes without saying that you will need to supply your flock with daily fresh food and water.

Daily, you should always glance at your chickens to make sure that they all look and act healthy. Novices may be surprised at how quickly your favorite hen can spiral downhill. If you notice one chicken that is not quite right, there is no shame in separating her from the rest of the flock while you put in a call to your veterinarian.

There seems to be some debate on what you should do after collecting your hen's eggs, but you never need to wash them until you are ready to use them (unless they are, well, poopy). This is because when eggs are laid, their shells possess a nearly invisible natural coating referred to as *bloom*, and this coating will keep air and bacteria out of the egg. This is nature's way of keeping the egg fresher for a longer period of time. This may seem like a difficult thing to grasp, but as long as you don't wash your eggs, there is no need to refrigerate them. Did you know that the United States is one of the only countries where eggs are refrigerated?

One day out on the counter at room temperature will be equal to a week in the refrigerator. The rule of thumb is that an egg will last longer if you refrigerate them, so if you have more eggs than you can consume within a week, you will want to refrigerate them. However, if you practice washing your eggs as soon as you collect them, then you should refrigerate them immediately. Store your eggs pointy side down to keep them fresher longer. If you have a backlog of eggs, you may find it helpful to mark your eggs lightly with a pencil to keep track of the dates they were collected.

This rule of thumb, however, only applies to your backyard eggs and not the store-bought variety. Through processing, the bloom has already been removed from these eggs, so they will always need to be refrigerated. The same rule will apply to any eggs that have already been refrigerated—once in the fridge, they should stay in the fridge!

If you want to leave your eggs out, you can leave them in a bowl on the counter and rinse them off with some warm water prior to being used. If at any time you feel unsure about one of your eggs, you can always perform the float test.

The Egg Float Test

Let's face it; if you have a sizable flock, you may find that sometimes the eggs will take on a life of their own, and you will be left with a sizable amount of them. You may even miss one tucked in the corner of your favorite hen's nesting box, and you wonder how long that's been there. Perhaps you own a sneaky hen who has hidden some eggs under one of your bushes, and the time frame of when they were laid may be unknown. Yard eggs are perfectly acceptable as long as they aren't cracked.

If you are worried about an egg's freshness, or lack thereof, you can perform the egg float test. To do this, fill a tall glass with warm water. If you use cold water and there is any bacteria present, the chill could cause it to be drawn into the egg. Gently drop your egg into the glass and pay attention to what your egg does next.

- If fresh, an egg will lie flat on the bottom of the glass.

- An egg that is one to two weeks old will start to rise off the bottom of the glass.

- If your egg in question is two months old or thereabouts, you will notice that the egg will be standing straight up, and the pointy end will be touching the bottom of the glass.

- Any egg that is older than three months or floats to the top of the glass is considered bad and should be thrown out.

The reason an egg rises is because air has seeped in through the pores of the eggshell, causing the air sac inside the egg to enlarge and dry out the egg. This will cause one end of the egg to rise. You should note too, that an egg will start losing nutrients as it ages, but it will still be perfectly good to consume. Once you have put your eggs in water, you have removed the natural bloom, and if you are keeping it, you should refrigerate it or use it immediately. Older eggs often peel better if you hard-boil them (and add a dash of salt). Keep to the old adage; when in doubt, throw it out.

Can you test an egg without placing it in water? Some say that you can shake an egg, and should you hear sloshing inside, the egg has probably gone bad. If you are worried about a certain egg, always break it separately in a bowl instead of directly into the dish you are preparing. If it smells bad, looks discolored, or cloudy, you should throw it away.

Tips for Collecting Clean Backyard Eggs

While you may or may not choose to store your eggs on the counter, no one wants to look at messy or dirty eggs, so here are a few tips we can share with you to keep it clean!

- When possible, do not allow your hens to sleep in the nesting boxes. It's true; chickens will poop even when they are asleep. With chickens instinctively looking for the highest place to sleep, you should always place your roosts higher than your nesting boxes. If you have a stubborn hen who insists on sleeping in her box, lift her out and place her on a roost after dark in an attempt to condition them to roost. Should she persist, you may need to block off the boxes during the late afternoon once your hens have laid their eggs.

- Every morning, change the bedding in your nesting boxes. By making it part of your morning routine, it will be simple to fluff your hen's bedding and keep it clean.

- Keep your nesting boxes on the wall that is opposite the coop door. By making your hens walk all the way across the coop, they might hopefully shed any mud or excess dirt they have on their feet.

- Persuade your broody hens to stop sitting on non-fertile eggs. If you don't have a rooster, then your eggs will not be fertilized, and your broody hens don't need to be sitting on them. By hogging a nest, your broody hen may have other hens start picking on her, which can result in the broody hen being injured, broken eggs, or egg eating. Some methods to discourage a broody hen are

  - To collect any eggs from her as soon as possible, even if you need to collect a few times a day.

  - Gently, remove your broody hen from her chosen nest and carry her to the far end of your chicken habitat, where you have scattered some of her favorite treats.

  - Remove her from the nest and place her on a roosting bar after dark.

  - Place a frozen water bottle in the nest she covets.

  - Block her chosen nest.

- You should collect your eggs regularly to help protect them from predators.

Daily Needs

In addition to providing fresh food and clean water, you should lock your chickens up every night in order to keep them safe from any predators in the area. Keep an eye on your flock's pecking order since an ill chicken may cause a change in her status within the group.

When your hens are laying, they may need to add an additional level of calcium to help make strong eggshells. To aid your hens, you should provide a separate dish with cracked oyster shells. This will serve as a natural supplement to your feed. Serving this free choice allows your chickens to only take what they need instead of putting it in with your feed.

If you are new to chickens, you will probably be overwhelmed at how much and how often your bird poops. There is no denying it; chickens require a lot of cleanup effort. When you multiply that by the number of birds you own, you will need a plan in place on how you plan to deal with all the poop.

Frequent Needs

Even chickens need to be groomed. We already explained the importance of dust baths, but you will have to also keep an eye on their nails and their feet. Watch for ulcers on their footpads as these can lead to other problems, like lameness or infection.

Keep your chickens separated during transport. These can be cat carriers or cages and have holes for proper ventilation. Your chickens should be able to sit comfortably, and you can cushion the box with some soft bedding. You should also take along some food and water so that you can make a few stops during the trip to eat and drink.

Monthly Coop Care

For the best results in cleanliness, you should change the bedding in the chicken coop monthly. Failure to clean your coop monthly could result in an ammonia build-up, which can cause respiratory illness. Some people have used a hack consisting of placing dropping boards under the roosting poles to speed clean up the morning. By doing this, you can lift out the trays, hose them off and place them back inside for the next night.

Twice a Year

It's a great idea to completely clean your chicken coop from top to bottom every six months. What this means is that you not only will remove all the bedding, nests, and feed containers, but you will scrub them down with the preferred solution of one part bleach, one part dish soap, and ten parts water. After washing down everything, rinse them, and then allow them to dry thoroughly before rebedding or replacing food and water containers.

Want to keep the chemicals out of your coop? You can mix up this all-natural coop cleaner!

Ingredients

- 6 grapefruit or 8 oranges or 12 limes or lemons

- Apple cider vinegar

- Glass jar

- Refillable spray bottle

Directions

1. Clean out the juice and insides of the fruits you have chosen to use. Hopefully, you have something in mind to use these for since this recipe utilizes only the skins of the fruit.

2. Place the fruit skins into a large jar (with an air-tight lid) and add apple cider vinegar until the skins are completely submerged.

3. Find an out-of-the-way place for this to sit and ferment for the length of two weeks.

4. Once those two weeks are up, grab a strainer and empty the contents of the jar through it. You will keep the liquid and discard the skins.

5. Use equal parts of water and solution in your sprayer, and the best part is that you can use it as a cleaner in your home as well!

Seasonal Chicken Care

You have done the research and selected the correct breeds based upon your geographical location, but there are a couple of things that you may have to do for seasonal care.

Chickens are usually able to adapt to cold weather changes, but you may need to rub petroleum jelly on their wattles and combs to protect your flock from frostbite. You should have a plan in place to make sure that your chicken's water supply doesn't freeze. If you live in a colder climate, you should have electricity in your coop so that you can use a water heater. Even though it's cold, make sure that there are no drafts present. The presence of a draft can result in illness in even the healthiest of chickens. You may want to shield them with some plastic sheeting surrounding their coop or even their yard.

Overheating is also a danger to your flock, and that is why you need to provide them with shade and ventilation. Times of extreme heat can be a stressor to your birds, so don't be surprised when their egg production drops until temperatures regulate.

Here Come the Rodents

One big thing that people aren't always prepared for is rodent control. There are always mice, rats, chipmunks, and squirrels around, but they can become a huge problem quickly. One way to try and deter them is to use an invasive plant such as mint. It's a quick-growing plant that replicates quickly, and rodents just hate the smell.

Chicken Predators Are Relentless

You have your coop and yard all planned out, and you feel that you have crossed every T and dotted every I until a predator strikes. Every potential predator will notice that you have a new addition, and they will be not only checking out your flock, but they will also be studying how to attack them. The persistence of these predators will frustrate and surprise you with how intelligent they can be.

It's heartbreaking to open your coop door and find out that your flock has been wiped out, so to keep your chickens safe, you will need to predator-proof your coop. You may think that traps or your trusty shotgun might be the best solution, but it can be illegal to seek this kind of revenge. Plus, if you have a coop on a small acreage, trust me, your neighbors will not take kindly to the use of a gun.

Your best defense against chicken predators is to keep a sturdy and tight coop that will make entry impossible. Were you aware that a mink can squeeze through a one-inch diameter hole? Did you also know that weasels can fit through something even smaller? Here are a few ways to predator-proof your coop at night.

- Just before dusk, close and latch all coop doors.

- Use a strong mesh wire to cover all your windows. Do not employ chicken wire because a raccoon can tear through that wire like a hot knife through butter. A one-half-inch square hardware wire will keep out the raccoons and the minks too.

- Use concrete, calking, wire, or expanding foam to fill in any holes or large cracks that form around doors, windows, or in walls.

- Walk around the perimeter of your yard and coop and look for any indication that something has been trying to dig under the coop walls or yard enclosures. You can bury mesh at least one foot deep around the sides of your chicken coop and yard, which will deter predators from digging.

- Do you have piles of firewood, brush piles, or other things on your property in which predators can successfully hide? You are going to want to eliminate any of those potential havens for chicken enemies.

- Install motion detector lights that can startle potential predators as they approach.

- Never leave uneaten food lying around to attract predators. You should always clean up the excess and store any chicken food in air-tight, odor-free containers.

You will have an entirely new set of challenges for the daytime predators who also would love nothing more than to snatch a quick bite to eat. Surprisingly, neighborhood dogs are large chicken killers, but you also have to worry about the predators from above, like hawks, owls, and eagles. There are weasels, minks, and foxes that are out hunting during the day, but it is rare to see a raccoon, opossum, or skunk unless it is at least dusk. Some measures that you can take during the day are found below.

- A sturdy fence will keep your chickens in and thwart the neighborhood dogs and foxes, but not coyotes. A decent height would be about four feet tall. This will keep in your heavier chicken breeds, but if you have some chickens that are smaller in stature, you will want a six or eight-foot fence in place.

- Electric poultry fencing can be a good option against ground predators.

- Provide your flock with some overhead protection. If you want to keep the raptors from diving out of the sky to snatch up your precious flock members, then you will want to cover your runs with wire mesh. If an overhead mesh is not practical for you, then make sure that you give your chickens somewhere to hide not only from predators but the hot sun. Plant a few shrubs or give them something like a picnic table for cover.

Chicken owners can be lulled into a false sense of security when no attempts by predators are made for months, but then suddenly, your whole flock is gone. You would be amazed at how quickly a lot of birds can be wiped out. Prevention is the only way to keep them safe. If you have taken all these measures and are still plagued by wildlife predators, you may need a licensed wildlife trapping service.

You can bet if there is a puzzle, even a complicated one, neighborhood raccoons will figure it out. And if they can't, they are known to pull a chicken's head through the wire mesh in place and leave the body behind. You are not the only one around that loves a good chicken dinner! You will have to outwit many of these following predators.

- Foxes
- Coyotes
- Raccoons
- Bobcats
- Opossums
- Skunks
- Weasels
- Squirrels
- Bears
- Neighborhood dogs
- Neighborhood or feral cats
- Minks
- Owls
- Hawks

- Eagles

- Cats

- Snakes

- Rats

How to Introduce Your Own Dogs to Your Flock

Above, we talked about neighborhood dogs, but what about your own dogs and how they will react to your newest additions? The key is to start with short introductions, and hopefully, you have a well-trained dog that will listen to the sit and stay commands. While your chickens are protected inside the confines of their coop, this is a perfect time to make that first introduction to Fido. Take your dog near the bird enclosure, so each of the species has time to see and smell each other. Continue these short-timed introductions until they seem to accept each other and remain calm.

Once this step proves successful, you can try holding a chicken while your dog is secured and see what kind of reaction you receive. If both remain calm, your next step is to try letting your birds free-range in an area and bring your dog out on a leash. Watch their responses to each other. Each animal has a different response time so give your dog and chickens a chance to be comfortable while having the other around. If you see that things are progressing and there are no negative responses, then you can try a supervised mixer between species.

It is important to take your time because this is a huge adjustment for your dog, and you should know that some dogs will never mix well with chickens. Let your dog know if they are not behaving properly, just like you would if they were refusing to sit or stay. There are some breeds of dogs that have a prey drive and are bred specifically to hunt, and you should realize that this may never be overcome. Your dog should never be allowed to ingest any of the chicken's food or water because they, too, are susceptible to salmonella, and this could make them very ill. If you are using a medicated feed for your chickens, you should be aware that this can also make your dog sick.

Both dogs and chickens can live in harmony. Just take things slow, and should your dog not want to be friends with your chickens, don't be upset with your dog. Sometimes you just can't undo generations of characteristics.

Plan for a Place to Keep Ill Birds

You think that you will never have a sick bird, but then you observe Pricilla, and she looks a bit off. Now, you wish you had planned on an isolation area or sickbay.

It's a common theme when chicken owners reflect on their humble beginnings, that they had all wished they had taken time to plan better and calculated expenses better when they first started. Building a coop and run is not something you want to do twice! Take into account the costs and all the wonderful new inventions that you can equip your coop with, but you may want to skip the widescreen television and the satellite dish.

- Automatic chicken doors
- Chicken swings
- Water base heater
- Goodnature rat and mouse trap
- Electric poultry netting
- Chicken clothing
- Roll out nesting boxes
- Incubator
- Brooder

Chickens Love to Dig

If your goal is to free-range your chickens, you need to know that your property will suffer from the march of the chickens. You may think that it's cool to watch your chickens dig, scratch, and peck at the soil in search of a tasty insect or grubworm, but you should be prepared to watch your vegetables, fruits, and expensive landscape plants fall victim to your chickens' path of discovery. They love nothing more than the challenge of unpotting your potted plants and consuming all your new sprouts of grass you are attempting to grow after last year's march of the chickens.

Besides hunting in the soil, chickens will consume a large number of inedible objects too, so if your yard has pieces of Styrofoam, wood, plastic, glass, nails, or other foreign objects, you might find that they will eat these right alongside your cherry tomatoes.

Zoonosis

If you are unfamiliar with this term, this is what a disease that can be transferred from animal to human is called. While the risk from chickens is rated low, very low, or extremely low, you should still be aware that they exist. Usually, both campylobacter and salmonella are caused by not cooking chicken or their eggs properly. However, all live fowl carry salmonella germs in their guts. Your poultry can have the salmonella germs present in their droppings, which can transmit to their feathers, feet, and even their beaks. As your chickens walk around their coop, they can contaminate their coops, cages, bedding, feed, and water dishes. This is why keeping everything clean is so very important. We encourage you to wear gloves and wash your hands immediately after handling chickens and their surroundings.

The categories with the most risk are children younger than the age of five, adults over the age of 65, or people that have weakened immune systems. Below are some basic rules to follow when handling any kind of poultry.

- Poultry should be kept outdoors. While it might be tempting to allow your favorite chicken to roam around your home, they can spread salmonella germs to your home surfaces.

- Always wash your hands thoroughly with soap and water after handling your chickens, their eggs, or anything within their domain, like feeders or waterers. If you don't have a place readily accessible to soap and water, use some hand sanitizer.

- Do not snuggle, kiss, or hold your live poultry near your face (besides salmonella exposure, they could peck you, and that hurts). You should also avoid eating or drinking in the chicken enclosure.

- Cook your eggs thoroughly until both the white and the yolk are firm.

- Only clean your poultry equipment outside of the home. All cages, feed, or water containers should be cleaned outside of the home. One of the best things that you can do is to dedicate a single pair of shoes to wear while performing your poultry chores, and you would be wise to keep them outside of the home.

- Children under five years of age, adults over 65, or people with weakened immune systems should avoid handling live poultry. Younger children are most at risk because their immune systems are still in development, and they are far more likely to stick their fingers in their mouths. Anyone with a severe immune disease is especially at risk for salmonella.

Avian flu or bird flu is monitored closely by the Department of Agriculture, and to date, there has never been a single case of avian flu in the United States. It is thought that, should there ever be an outbreak, it will most likely come from a large commercial flock and not from a smaller-scale, backyard operation. Most of the cases reported in the world are usually based in Asia or the Middle East and involve children handling sick or diseased chickens.

We never even considered this, but just in case it comes up during some dinner party conversation when you cannot stop talking about chickens, chickenpox has absolutely nothing to do with chickens. The original reason that this disease was so named was that the blisters were thought to look like chickpeas.

Children & Chickens

Young children may not realize how fragile a newly hatched chick is and should not be allowed to hold them for both their sakes. Raising chickens can be a marvelous educational tool, but you need to know that your children are educated before handling any of the chicks or chickens, and you would follow the same rules that you would for them handling a newborn puppy or kitten.

Raising children together with chickens can enrich their lives, bringing them an understanding of food production and responsibility. Given time, children will experience some unforgettable life lessons and may even develop an interest in showing chickens through their local 4-H group.

There are some common-sense avenues to follow while your children share their lives with chickens.

- Pick out some child-friendly breeds. In Chapter 3, we gave you a list of some great starter breeds for your new venture and made comments to those breeds considered child friendly.

- If possible, you should pick out your chicks together, but since many come via mail order that may not always be possible.

- Teach your children the correct way to hold chicks and make sure that they understand how fragile they are.

- Pick out names for your new chicks.

- Build a chicken coop and discuss all the options for keeping your chickens safe and happy.

- Watch your chickens grow through that gawky teenage stage.

- Have a celebration when your new chicks grow old enough to lay their first egg.

- Practice safe chicken handling and practice biosecurity rules.

- **Wash hands!**

What's the Tab?

So, how much does it cost to raise some chickens? Prices change from year to year, so we have included a blank chart to follow, but you are going to want to figure out a five-year cost, add that up, and then divide it by 60 months to get an average cost per month. Of course, this cannot include any medical costs because there is no way to know how much that may or may not be.

Item	Approximate 5 Year Cost
A Hand-Made Chicken Coop for # of Chickens	$
Fencing Costs	$
Chicken Feed	$
Bedding	$
Cost of # of Chickens	$

Coop Supplies: Feeders, Waterers, etc.	$

Add your costs together, then divide by 60 months, and you should come out with a cost per month on your chicken venture. *Tip: Calculate on the high side to be safe. This way, if it ends up averaging a bit less, you will be happy. Adding more chickens and keeping them longer can drive your per month cost down.*

Despite all these concerns, most chicken owners would not only do it all again; they would have done it sooner. Why? Because chickens are cool!

Chapter 5:
If You Build it, They Will Come

Your chickens will need a coop, and this is going to be the biggest and most important item you will struggle with. Designs are extremely personal, and you want to make sure that you have done everything just right, so you won't experience any regrets. How large you should make it is going to depend on how well you do chicken math.

There is an old saying that ingenuity is the mother of invention, and you only have to browse the internet a bit to find some truly innovative ways to set up a coop while not taxing your budget. Even if you are on a strict budget, the chicken coop will be the most important investment when it comes to safely raising your chickens. Truthfully, if you are lacking in carpentry skills, there are still some impressive, prefabricated buildings out there for you to purchase.

Tips for First-Time Builders

We would be remiss if we didn't tell you about some big mistakes that first-time coop builders make, so before we get into construction, you should probably consider some of the following points.

Plan Out Everything

The devil is in the details, so plan out everything before you build. After choosing a suitable plan, make sure that you select materials that are readily available and easy to work with. Doors should open inward, and you will want to take into consideration that your chickens will need lots of fresh air since they still spend a considerable amount of time in the coop, even if they are free-range. Sliding windows will help provide them with some cool summer breezes.

Keeping your floors clean is very important, and you will need to cover them with materials to keep your chickens busy digging and scratching even when they are cooped up. In addition, your floors should slope slightly toward the door in case you ever need to hose the coop out, leaving you with a clean coop and not lingering puddles.

Good Ventilation and Insulation Are a Must

Any farm building that houses livestock needs good ventilation, and a chicken coop is no exception. You want free movement of air but no drafts. Without the benefit of air movement, you will risk a buildup of high carbon monoxide and humidity levels. Your chickens will be uncomfortable and stressed, which will cause them to lay fewer eggs, and it can also promote the growth of mold in your coop and within the walls.

Insulate your walls. This helps your flock stay cool in the summer and warm in the winter. Insulation helps to regulate humidity levels inside the coop and will keep your chickens healthier.

Food and Water Placement Matters

Proper placement of the feeders and waterers is important and should be raised to about the height of a chicken's back. The reasoning for this is very simple: your chickens can reach up a bit to get their food and water, but they cannot get their feet in it. There is nothing more frustrating than setting out clean feeders and waterers only to have your chickens hop in and start scratching and pooping. Make sure that feeders and waterers are far away from roosts so that they don't get pooped in.

Chickens and Leftovers

Your chickens can eat a lot of your kitchen leftovers, but you should be sure to remove anything left uneaten from their coop. Any remaining pieces may mold or decay, bringing bacteria to your chicken's home, which could make them ill or bring rodents and predators. Food scraps should be limited and add up to 10% or less of their daily intake.

Not everything is going to be safe to give to your chickens, and some can even be deadly. Below, we have listed some common food leftovers that you should never give to your birds.

- Dry beans and lentils

- Dry rice

- Avocado

- Apple seeds

- Chocolate

- Tomatoes

- Eggplants

- Onions

- Lettuce

- Spinach

- Rhubarb

- Mushrooms

- Coffee

- Tea

In addition to these, you should avoid feeding foods that have been fried or seasoned to be salty or sweet. Too much excess fat, sodium, or sugar can make your chickens sick. Even though we eat these, they aren't really good for us either, so don't give them to your flock.

Keep the Elements in Mind

Design your coop with a good light source in mind. If you face your coop south, they should receive maximum sunlight throughout the day. You should plan on installing a light in your coop for the winter months when days are shorter, and the sunlight is fleeting. Added light in the winter will also help to keep your egg production flowing, and your chickens will remain happy.

Coops should always protect your flock from the elements. Think of this as their home, and just like yours, it should be properly sealed against drafts. Don't forget that your coop should be elevated to keep out the dampness. When it rains, your coop should remain dry.

Predatory Dangers

Your coop should also protect your flock from predators. We already talked about this in the previous chapter, but look over those points so that you can keep your flock safe. After a predator attack, you should keep the flock cooped for a few days.

Always perform a bed check. Then, every night, count your chickens to ensure that some broody hen isn't hiding in the bushes, making her vulnerable to an attack from predators.

This may not be an obvious strategy, but if any friend visits with their dogs, they should always be leashed. Nothing is going to kill a friendship faster than having their dog kill your favorite chicken right in front of you.

Have a Poop Plan!

This may sound ridiculous to you, but when you install your roosts, there are some ways to thwart all the nighttime chicken droppings. It can be as simple as placing older cookie sheets underneath them at night and hosing them off each morning, leaving your bedding clean and ready for the next day.

Size Matters

Build it big enough. If you have plans of ever adding more chickens at a future date, always build a little bigger than your original plans.

Building a Coop

Gosh, where to start! There are so many directions to travel in regard to your coop. Just remember to build the hen house before you bring your chickens home to roost.

Prefab

There are many pre-built chicken coop designs that it can be tough to pick just one. When deciding, make sure that you keep your climate in mind. Prices can vary, but you can expect to pay anything from around $170 to $8,000, depending on what you want to spend.

- Apex house designs are proven and less expensive than other designs. They have wire floors that can stop both predators and your chickens from digging.

- Rectangular houses typically have a sloping roof to the coop and a flat top over the run area. The roofs are either sliding or hinged for easy access. These are usually raised over a section of your chickens' run, which can make it easier to clean, feed, and collect eggs.

Elevated chicken coops are typically around two feet off the ground, and your chickens can make their way in through a small ladder. While this is not a coop built for cold winters, if you live in a warmer area, this will keep burrowing animals out, and when placed in a run, this will provide your flock with some extra protection from the elements. Raised coops are usually a stationary construct, but some designs can lend themselves to add some wheel attachments, making them mobile. If you choose not to rotate areas, your chickens will likely turn the patch underneath their coop into their dust bath area.

These ready-made hen houses always look great in a catalog, but, if possible, you should try to see them in person. Be objective and determine if you can clean it out without having to dismantle the whole kit and caboodle. Does it seem sturdy? A raised structure can be easier to clean and collect eggs, but they can be top-heavy. If you live in an area with windstorms, you don't want your girls in danger. Always read online reviews of the product to see what other people have to say about the model and learn from their experiences.

While stationary homes tend to be a bit larger, the smaller units can be movable. If you opt for a movable house and run, you should plan on moving it about every three days as a minimum; more often is ideal. The concept is to never let your grass get too worn down. The aid of a tractor can move some larger portable coops and runs, but these can house as many as 25 chickens, and by the time you climb to a flock of that size, you are considered a serious chicken owner and should consider building something more permanent.

Many first-time chicken owners opt to begin with a prefabricated coop as a starting off point when deciding if chicken ownership is right for them. Once you are hooked, you can always design your own.

Build it Yourself

If you are handy or perhaps have a really good friend that can swing a hammer with the best of them, you can make the chicken coop of your dreams. If you can build a coop, make sure that you add an equally wonderful run to keep your flock happy and healthy. Regardless of how *eggstravagant* you make your custom coop, you will still need to include all the basic niceties for your flock. Keeping it safe and functional doesn't mean that it has to be boring. Follow your muse and add some style!

If you don't own a lot of tools, don't worry, it doesn't take many tools to build your coop, just a few common hand and power tools, and you will be all set. If you have to borrow tools from a friend, make sure that you invite them over to help. All you have to do is to promise to give them some fresh eggs, and most will be delighted to help. Make sure you offer them snacks and refreshments for the duration of the project.

Many of these tools you probably have laying around the house anyway and may depend upon the kind of coop you are planning to build. Here are a few tools you will need to create your coop.

- Safety gear like work gloves, hearing protection, and protective goggles.

- Tape measure

- L ruler

- Circular saw

- Hammer

- Drill

- Levels. Preferably a pocket-sized, two-foot, and four-foot model.

- Speed square

- Tin snips, because there is bound to be some wire involved somewhere in your coop or run.

When building your chicken coop, make sure that you take your time to think things through. If you are looking for ideas to incorporate, take a look at premade plans to see if they have any groundbreaking ideas that you want to include.

Write down all your steps and ideas. By doing this, you will be able to make a detailed list of all the materials and equipment you will need. Remember that cramped birds are unhappy, so the bigger the space, the better!

Repurposing

Perhaps your property already has an unused shed that you can repurpose? Conversion can be a fun project, and you can design the interior any way that you wish. This can save you a lot of time and materials since the shell is already there and all you need to do is customize it. When modifying an existing building, make sure to raise the flooring off the ground to prevent any possibilities of flooding or rotting of floorboards. You may need to also redesign the ventilation of the shed.

Have an old childhood playhouse on the property? This might also make a really cute coop! Tired of your she-shed? It can still be repurposed for chicks! Maybe you have access to some architectural salvage or even an old unused silo? You can decorate these any way you want too! There is no reason you can't make it look metropolitan, country chic, or even hang an old chandelier from the ceiling. The point is you can make anything that suits your tastes. We bet if you google custom chicken coops, you can come up with about 20 that you love. Just remember to consider your climate when you design your dream coop.

Nesting Boxes

It can be infuriating to build a dozen nesting boxes, and five hens will crowd into just one box! Don't laugh; it happens, especially since hens will often have favorite boxes in which to deposit their eggs. When figuring out how many nesting boxes you will need, plan on one box for every three to four hens. If you put them at floor level, they will not use them, so make sure they are always a few feet off the ground. The only exception to this might be if you have a breed that doesn't fly, such as a Silkie. They may prefer a ground-level box.

If possible, your nesting boxes should be in a darker area of your coop for privacy, far from feeding stations, and not directly underneath any roosts. If you are fortunate enough to have a spacious coop, you can put nesting boxes in a few different places. You can even place one or two out in the run; just make sure that you collect those eggs before any predators beat you to them.

If you are just starting out, you may find that you need to train your hens in the use of nesting boxes. When they start laying, which is somewhere around the 16-20 weeks of age, you may notice them wandering and looking restless. You can gently guide them to a nest that contains fake eggs or golf balls in the nest. If you have older hens, the younger ones will follow their lead and use a nesting box. Should they need some added incentive, you may need to sprinkle some cracked corn in the boxes, but make sure you keep the nests clean and fresh. If there is poop or dirt in it, they will not use it. Remember earlier in this book, we recommended that you close off these boxes at night so that your chickens won't poop in them and on the eggs. You may find that you have a hen that refuses to use nesting boxes, and you will never change their mind no matter what you do, so don't let it frustrate you.

Hens prefer a clean and cozy nesting box to lay her eggs in. If you don't want to build them, there are several you can purchase from farm stores or online. Just as there are plans online for your coop, there are do-it-yourself plans for nesting boxes as well. The size of your boxes is going to depend on the size of your chickens.

- Bantam chickens tend to prefer smaller boxes, roughly 10 x 12 x 10 inches

- Standard chicken size boxes are 12 x 12 x 12 inches

- Larger breeds need a bit more wiggle room, so plan on 12 x 14 x 12 inches

The preferred materials for nesting boxes are either wood, metal, or plastic since both are easy to maintain and wash. When attaching them to your coop walls, remember that wooden boxes are considerably heavier than plastic ones, so you should have some study walls or supports to hold them in place.

Some chicken owners are very creative when it comes to nesting boxes, and there are examples using wine barrels, five-gallon buckets, plastic milk crates, and even a nest built out of a covered tote.

Granted, some hens often decide to lay their eggs outside, under a large bush, but that makes them hard to retrieve, and predators will beat you to them.

If you are doing something of your own design, you may be able to build nesting boxes that you can access from outside of the coop as well as the inside.

When deciding upon nesting materials, below are a few popular choices. To cover all the hens' choices, you may want to vary what's in your boxes, so they have a choice.

- Pine shavings
- Straw
- Nesting pads (these are washable and inexpensive)
- Pine needles
- Leaves
- Sawdust

Roosting Bars

Roosts are elevated bars that are roughly two to four inches wide, and every coop needs them. They can be made from natural branches, narrow planks, ladders, or long wooden rods, and you should allow at least eight inches of space per hen. Metal bars can be harder to grip and be slippery, especially for an older chicken with arthritis. If you are in a region with cold winters, they could get frostbitten feet.

Chickens will instinctively perch at night, preferring to get off the ground as far as possible, so they remain out of the reach of predators. By sleeping up high, your chickens are also kept from sleeping on the floor of the coop, where they may be lingering bacteria or external parasites.

Having roost bars is highly recommended to keep your flock happy and stress-free. Roosts also allow your submissive birds to avoid their more dominant flockmates. Your bar length and sturdiness may vary depending upon whether you have a flock of bantams or one composed of Jersey Giants and how large your flock is.

You will want to position your bars so that they do not block any entrances, away from feeders, waterers, or nesting boxes, so keep them all clean. In addition, you do not want to position them in front of any ventilation areas in case of winter frostbite.

To appeal to your chickens, these can be placed as close as 18 inches from your coop's ceiling. If you have baby chicks, you can provide a small roosting bar in the brooder.

Dropping Board

This is a collective term that is used to describe placing a board below your chicken's roosts to catch those bedtime poops. This practice enables you to clean daily with ease. The whole idea of a dropping board is so that you clean that more and your coop less. It should just take a few minutes each day.

This isn't a new idea, but the concept leaves the execution open for interpretation. You can literally use anything that your chickens won't be able to tear apart, but there are a few things to keep in mind.

- It should be wide enough to catch all the droppings that fall from your roosting area.

- If you are using a wooden board, you can cover it with something easier to clean, such as scrap linoleum or peel and stick tiles.

- Trays can be filled with sand or Sweet PDZ to make it easier to scoop or scrape.

- It is helpful to have edges to hold the litter (and the poop) in until you can clean and remove it for use the next night.

- Whatever you use, it should be easy to remove for deep cleaning.

Besides making your cleaning chores easier, using a dropping board can have a few other benefits.

- Moisture will be reduced in the coop, which will keep your flock cleaner, healthier, and warmer.

- It will help with a reduction in ammonia, which can damage your chicken's respiratory systems. It can cut down on other odors as well.

- Reduces flies during the warm summer months.

- By keeping your coop clean, you will save money on bedding and also reduce how frequently you need a full coop cleaning.

- By observing overnight droppings, you may be able to identify an illness early.

Without the daily removal of the overnight poops, odor and flies can become a problem. You can quickly clean up a dropping board by removing it and hosing it off.

You can build your very own dropping board! Here's how.

Tools:

- Tape measure
- Pencil
- Handsaw

- Table or circular saw

- Drill with screwdriver bits

- Sandpaper

Materials:

- Plywood - since this will be used as the base of your tray, it should be wide enough to cover the drop zone of your chicken's nightly poops. Ideally, you want it to span the width, but if you have a sizable coop, you may want it in a few sections for more ease of handling.

- 1 x 2 or similar cuts of wood. These boards will be used to create the needed edges of your dropping board. You will need enough to cover the length of your board or boards.

- Vinyl tile or sheet vinyl

- Vinyl glue

- Screws

- Scrap wood to make supports for the dropping board while inside the coop.

Directions:

1. You will need to take your coops layout into account when deciding what size to make your dropping boards and keep them easy to handle.

2. If you don't own power saws or are uncomfortable using them, take time to pre-measure everything you will need to construct your drop boards and have the local home improvement store cut them for you. Some may charge a fee, but most will do this for no additional cost.

3. After the plywood is cut to the correct size, use sandpaper to smooth the edges and remove any hazard of splinters.

4. Measure and cut two pieces of the 1 x 2's and make them about two inches shorter than the length of your plywood board. Again, sand the edges to remove the risk of splinters.

5. Screw these pieces to the outer edges of your plywood piece, keeping the outside edges flush, and one end of the board should also be flush with these pieces (you will only frame the long sides making it easier to slide the boards in and out of your coop and to clean).

6. If you are using stick tiles, measure, cut, and install them on the tray you have just created. Should you decide to use sheet vinyl, you can trim any excess after it has been glued on.

7. If you want to elevate the trays, you can cut four blocks of your scrap wood to match the measurements of the short end of your tray and

attach them to your coop sides so you can slide your tray in and out underneath a roost. Ideally, your tray should sit under the roost and be about halfway between the roost and the floor. These two boards will make it simple for you to slide the tray in and out for cleaning. Attach these boards using some screws.

8. You can fill your drop board with sand or sweet PDZ to help cut down on the smell in the coop. You do not need to use a lot, just enough to help clump us the droppings.

Tip: Remember that wood is subject to expanding and contracting depending upon the levels of humidity in the air, so don't design it to fit tightly.

It is all going to depend on how clean you want to keep your coop. If you are a neat freak like us, you can pick the clumps off these boards every morning and perform a complete clean once or twice a week. In between cleanings, feel free to add a little litter if you feel it is low. Every few months, you should plan on cleaning out all the litter and giving it a full scrub with your homemade cleaner (see Chapter 4). Let it dry completely, replace the board with new litter, and you are ready to begin another week.

Enclosed Runs

Providing an enclosed run still allows your chickens to run around but stay safe from those predators that mean to do them harm.

Just like your coops, you have an option of shopping for prefabricated chicken runs that remind us of outdoor dog kennels. They are available online or at your local farm stores. However, you may want to build your own. Just make sure that you use heavy gauge wire (not chicken wire) and build it to keep your flock safe. Even if you think you have everything perfect, you may find yourself face to face with a possum or snake in your hen house.

Your first step is to determine the dimensions of your run and design it to incorporate your coop, which should be flush with one side of the run. A good rule of thumb for a small flock is a run approximately four feet in width. Personally, we would cover it too, but we have been told that a hawk would never land in this narrow space, but we would rather be safe than sorry.

Choose sturdy materials and recall that we mentioned earlier that a raccoon can reach through a wire fence and still kill a chicken.

Space your eight-foot posts about every six feet by using a post hole digger for the holes. After placing the posts in the hole, fill it up with dirt and pack with a tamper. Roll out the fence, and before attaching it to your posts, you should make certain that the fence is at ground level. Recall that earlier, we mentioned burying some wire fences for extra protection against predators. If you wish to do that, make a trench about six to 12 inches deep and once you place it in the trench, wrap one end around your first post and then use some zip ties to keep it in place while you continue to work.

Pull your fencing tightly against the rest of the posts and wrap the other end around your final post, also securing it with zip ties. Before you begin the final steps of stapling your fencing to the post, make sure that you are happy with how your project looks. If so, then use ¾ inch poultry staples to attach your fencing to the posts you have in place.

Don't forget to cut out an opening and install a gate so that you can enter the run. We like to leave nothing to chance, so if you want to cover your run, cover it with heavy-duty C Flex 80 round deer fencing, and you can secure this with zip ties. Make sure that you routinely walk your fence line, looking for attempts at digging or areas that may need repair.

Are There Plants to Avoid in Your Run or Garden Area?

You have put in a lot of hard work by now and are ready to bring your first flock of chickens home, but have you considered your landscaping? If you plan on giving your chickens free access outside of your run or if they are free-range, you should be aware of any potentially poisonous plants that may harm your chickens. Make sure you read through the list below and check if you have any of these plants in their environment. If so, you may want to remove these plants before they cause an illness.

Poisonous plants can be a tough thing for an average homeowner to identify. We understand that there are apps available on your phone that can identify a plant for you by merely uploading an image of what is growing in your yard. If you cannot locate one of those, perhaps you have a friend or neighbor that has a green thumb. They may be able to tell you which plants are which. If you are still in doubt, you can check out books on plant identification from your local library or your local bookstore. Besides this list of plants, there can be some seasonal growth for you to combat. Keep an eye out for seeds, pods, or acorns that could cause your chickens some danger, and never feed them anything that has been treated with chemicals.

The list We have compiled below may only refer to a part of the plant, their seeds, or at a certain stage of growth, so you should really read up on the plants you intend to landscape with or those already in the area of your coop. The first time your chickens sample some of these plants may not be critical, but if they continue to consume them, there may be a residual buildup. If any of these are near to your coop, you should rip them out.

- Azalea
- Black locust
- Bladderpod/bagpod
- Boxwood
- Buttercup
- Castor bean
- Cherry laurel
- Corn cockle
- Crown vetch
- Daffodil
- Daphne
- Death camas
- Ferns
- Foxglove
- Holly
- Honeysuckle
- Hydrangea
- Ivy
- Jasmine
- Jimsonweed/thornapple

- Lantana
- Lily of the valley
- Lupine
- Mexican poppy
- Milkweed
- Monkshood
- Mountain laurel
- Nightshade
- Oak leaves
- Oleander
- Poison hemlock
- Pokeberry
- Rattlebox
- Rhododendron
- Sweet pea
- Tobacco
- Tulip
- Water hemlock/cowbane
- Wisteria
- Yew

In addition to keeping an eye on these plants, you should keep any weeds pulled from around your coop and maintain a short grass border. Rodents love to hide in the deep weeds and grass, so this will keep them sneaking into your coop area.

Ideally, you should build a 12 to 18-inch border around your run made up of dirt or stone because the running of a lawnmower too close to your coop could stress out your birds. A lawnmower can be loud and scary to your chickens, but you may be able to make it fun for them by mowing so that your first pass will aim the grass cutting directly into the run. They will happily make a dash for it and enjoy the surprise green gifts. However, if you treat your lawn with harsh chemicals, do not give them to your chickens.

Chapter 6:
The World of Chickens Beyond Eggs

The majority of chicken owners begin their hobby for eggs, but there are more choices in the chicken world. You can choose to show, breed, or raise meat birds. There is no wrong answer, only the path you wish to follow.

In our case, we just love being surrounded by animals. It doesn't matter if they are dogs, horses, or chickens. Some of our best therapists never say a word.

Show Your Chickens

Being able to show your chickens is not just for 4-H and local poultry club shows. There are poultry shows you can attend to learn about new breeds, study up on bloodlines, and even get some answers as to how to enter the show ring yourself.

If you want to locate an exhibition close to you, visit the Poultry Show Central's website, where you can search by state and mark your calendar for any upcoming poultry show dates. You will want to follow the same protocols when visiting these shows that you would when entering your own coop. Consider the following:

- Disinfect your footwear before attending your home flock

- Bag your shoes before entering your vehicle for the ride home as a biosecurity measure

- Always wash your hands and use hand sanitizer frequently

- Wear extra layers of clothes so that if they become soiled, you can remove them

Since you will have your phone with you, you will be able to take photos, but don't forget to bring a pen and notepad to write important things down. There is always something to learn, and you never know what great piece of information or tips you will come across. Most of these shows will last a day or two, and you may want to sit in on any seminars offered.

While you are admiring those chickens, take some time to study any comments the judges may have made on the cage tags. If this is your first time attending a poultry show, just take it easy and soak it all in because this can be an alien but exciting experience. Below We have listed some of the abbreviations that you might find written on the judging tags.

- AOCCL - all other combs clean legged

- AOSB - all other standard breeds

- AOB - any other breed

- AOV - any other variety
- B, BT, BTM - bantam
- BB - best of breed
- BV - best of variety
- C - cock
- CH - champion
- CONT - continental
- DQ - disqualification
- H - hen
- K - cockerel
- LF - large fowl
- MED - Mediterranean
- OT - old trio
- P - pullet
- RCCL - rose comb clean legged
- RB - reserve of breed
- RC - rose comb
- RV - reserve of variety
- SCCL - single comb clean legged
- SC - single comb

- SF - standard fowl

- WF - waterfowl (ducks & geese)

- YT - young trio

If you are just getting into the poultry show world, take time to view all the different breeds because there are hundreds. Don't worry about asking questions because chicken owners *love* to talk about their birds! Most of them are always happy to share secrets and tips for up-and-coming competitors. New interest keeps their world thriving.

Preparing for a Show

If you want to participate in shows, always start by investing in quality birds from a reputable breeder.

The key to success is preparation, and there are some things you should do before your show.

- Wash your birds around a week prior to your show

- Groom your bird

- Clip nails & beaks

- Shine their feathers

- Clean their legs & feet

- Relax & enjoy

Several shows run a raffle to win items like feed or other poultry products, and with any luck, they may draw your name. If you are interested in purchasing stock, you should hang out in the sales area because this is the time some vendors will be willing to make a deal on pricing. If you do end up bringing new stock home, you should quarantine them for at least a month before letting them integrate with the rest of your flock.

The desire to show chickens is primarily focused on improving a breed, and it is an interesting hobby for people of all ages. Most shows are free to attend, but if there is a small charge, it is usually to help support the organization. Shows are filled with great people who love chickens and have common goals, so go, have fun and explore.

Breeding Your Chickens

Whether you want to show, or you just want to sell chicks perhaps to other backyard chicken owners, you'll still need to know a thing or two about breeding your chickens. We are sure that you know this, but without a rooster on the property, there is no way to fertilize a hen's egg to produce a chick. Below are some insights on breeding.

- Follow selective breeding habits. Most likely, you have a plan already in place to develop a certain breed. It doesn't matter if you just want to breed your favorite chickens or further a bloodline. What matters is that your birds should be healthy, exhibit good temperaments, and have good production.

- While chickens can produce fertilized eggs all year, they are most prolific during the springtime. This is especially true if you reside in a colder climate region since your flock will spend more energy staying warm than anything else.

- Keeping more than one rooster for your hens is usually not a good idea because it can create a lot of competition between them. It may be possible to have roosters together if they have been raised together and you provide them with at least 4 to 5 hens each. The one benefit of keeping more than a single rooster is that there is a higher fertility rate within your flock.

- If you choose to single out a rooster for breeding, you will need to remove any other roosters from the flock. Observe your rooster with his harem and make sure that he is doing his job.

- There is a wait time if you have just introduced a rooster to your flock. A hen's reproductive cycle will not produce a fertilized egg for at least two weeks.

- Keep an eye on your rooster to make sure that he isn't harming your hens with his spurs and beak.

It's normal for a rooster to jump on the hen's back and hold her in place by grabbing her comb. However, if you notice that your hens are losing feathers, appear stressed out, or looking bloody, your rooster might be overeager. If you are concerned about your hens, you can purchase a hen saddle to protect them, and when possible, trim your rooster's spurs and talons.

- If the rooster is harming your hens, you will have to decide to switch to a different rooster if you fear for your hen's physical or mental health. Without her, there will be no chicks.

- When your eggs are fertilized, you will start to notice them looking a bit different. If you see a small white splotch that puts you in mind of a bullseye, you will know that they are showing the signs of fertilization.

- Store your potential chicks at 50 to 60 degrees Fahrenheit for a week with the pointy end facing down. This is preferred to putting every egg into your incubator right away because this practice can cause some problems when it comes to hatching day. While in the incubator, your eggs need to be rotated and chicks removed when dry. This process can kill potential chicks that are still in the hatching process, so it is preferable to have all your eggs at the same stage of development.

There you go! Chicken breeding is not difficult. You just need to manage the safety of your girls and add all potential chicks to the incubator at the same time.

Hatching the Old-Fashioned Way

Many breeds of chickens make perfectly good mothers. However, sometimes, you may have a hen that doesn't want to sit on her eggs or raise her chicks. Now what? Luckily, you have had the foresight to add to your flock a couple of hens that are naturally broody and love nothing better than to sit on a nest of eggs.

If you are serious about breeding purebreds, then you may have those chickens separate from the rest or just start out with a flock of a single breed.

If your hen gets broody, don't make her feel uncomfortable about it. She needs to feel safe and protected, so she doesn't feel the need to abandon her eggs or chicks. During this time, you need to leave her eggs alone and place some food and water nearby. After hatching, your baby chicks will regulate their own temperature by positioning themselves under her, on her, or under her wings, depending upon the amount of heat they feel they need. You will still need to leave food and water nearby, and should you need to move them, try to do it in the evening when your hen is ready for sleep.

You should know that not all clutches of eggs will hatch even if the mother is dedicated. It is sad, but some chicks will either never make it out of their egg or pass away after hatching. After the first chicks hatch from the grouping, remove anything unhatched after four days have passed and *candle* them to check what is inside.

Candling Your Unhatched Eggs

You can check the inner contents of your hen's eggs by holding a light or lit candle near it. This process can help to determine if there is a chick in there ready to step into the world.

You should also candle the eggs that you are incubating to make sure that they are indeed fertilized and hold a growing chick inside. We suggest that you candle your eggs before placing them in the incubator initially. This can provide you with a comparison when you check them further. Any eggs with cracks do not necessarily need to be discarded, but you should monitor them closely. Unfertilized eggs will rot and begin to smell. It is also possible that any rotten eggs may burst and contaminate the other eggs in the incubator with bacteria.

You will need a bright light to look at your eggs, and the room you check them in should be dark. You can purchase a device at farm stores or cover the bright end of a flashlight with a piece of cardboard that you have fashioned a one-inch circular hole in.

When you are ready, pick up an egg and gently hold the larger end of the egg against the light, turning it slowly.

Avoid looking directly into the light but look inside the egg to determine if there is an embryo inside. Do not keep the egg against the light for very long because you don't want the embryo to become too hot.

Growing embryos can be easily identified by a roadmap of blood vessels during the first week. After that, you can probably see an eye or a shadow indicating a body. If you are lucky, you may even see some movement inside.

An embryo that stops growing will often show a red ring around the yolk. These should be removed from the incubator and thrown away as they are not fit to eat.

After checking over your eggs, gently place them back in their spot inside the incubator. Your incubated eggs should not be away from the incubator for more than 20 minutes.

You can keep a log to keep track of your observations and even place a number on each egg. If you are unsure about the contents of an egg, you can place it back in the incubator and check it again.

Generally, you should candle your average eggs when you place them in the incubator, again on day seven and then a third time on the fourteenth day. The general rule is to not candle them again from day 16 until the day of hatching because moving or shifting eggs during this stage could result in harming your chicks.

Raising Meat Chickens

So far, we have covered a lot of information about taking care of your chickens and what to do with all those wonderful eggs, but there is another industry in the chicken world, and that is the meat chicken. There are different rules when raising meat chickens as opposed to laying hens.

The best chickens to raise for meat are Cornish crosses; these are the big, white chickens that you will find in supermarkets and restaurants. They are efficiently bred to grow quickly, basically following eight weeks to your freezer.

These chickens are not overly bright and should be kept separate from any laying hens you have simply because they will be picked on and even killed by the other birds. They are not known to have much of a personality, and they do just one thing, eat. They will start and never stop, causing them to eat themselves to death.

According to Twain Lockhart (2020), feeding a meat bird is a bit different from your layers because they will need a diet that is higher in protein. The meat bird feed is designed to help build the bird's skeletal system to hold its weight. Because of the way these birds are engineered to gain weight, you should restrict their diet to 12 hours on, 12 hours off. If you don't, the birds may outgrow their legs too early and suffer from broken legs, and at around seven weeks of age, they may suffer heart attacks.

While it is true that some chicken breeds can double as both layer and meat birds, these may not prove profitable for a side business producing meat birds. We admit that it's true that it will cost less to just visit your local supermarket and purchase your chickens already processed for your dinner table, but there is nothing quite as satisfying as producing your own food at home. In addition, with chickens now being processed for the US market in China, consumers may feel safer knowing where their food is raised and how it is processed.

You should know that there are ordinances that may allow you to raise chickens but prohibit the actual slaughter within city limits. You may be able to network with another person outside of the city limits that already processes their birds, and for a fee, may process yours as well. You will be able to load up your freezer and enjoy the fruits of your labor all winter long.

Conclusion

By now, you have become completely immersed in the world of chickens, and we bet you just cannot wait to get started!

We began by explaining why you need chickens in your life and the many benefits that they bring to you and your family. After that, we covered how to keep your chickens happy, their behaviors, and how they communicate either with us or each other.

The ability to know your chickens inside and out will help you care for them and know about common illnesses and pests. In addition to these tips, we have provided a list of chicken breeds that are fantastic choices for new chicken owners and indicated which ones were especially kid friendly.

Not that it will keep you from owning your own flock, but we would be remiss if we didn't prepare you for all the things that accompany chicken ownership. We cannot stress enough how important it is to understand chicken math. This rule that governs the universe will determine the size of your coop and run.

Besides your coop cleaning chores, we have given you options on buying a coop, building one, or repurposing an existing building. And your coop would not be complete without a protective run enclosure, nesting boxes, roosting bars, and the ever-growing importance of a drop board that enables you to keep a cleaner coop.

The world of chickens is more than just a huge pile of eggs (although that's the most attractive reason to enter the chicken world). Beyond eggs, there is the show world, investing in refining a breed, or even raising meat chickens.

Hopefully, we have inspired you to invest some time when planning your new chicken operation. Whether it's three chickens or 300, you will find them entertaining and personable. We wish you the greatest experience in your chicken endeavors because life is better with chickens around!

References

5 tips for clean eggs from your backyard chickens. (n.d.). Fresh Eggs Daily. https://www.fresheggsdaily.blog/2013/05/coop-to-kitchen-5-tips-to-ensure-clean.html

8 simple tips for breeding chickens. (n.d.). www.thehappychickencoop.com. https://www.thehappychickencoop.com/8-simple-tips-for-breeding-chickens/

26 sounds that chickens make and what they mean. (2019, March 18). Flip Flop Ranch. https://flipflopranch.com/chicken-talk/

Alectryon (mythology). (2021, April 29). Wikipedia. https://en.wikipedia.org/wiki/Alectryon_(mythology)

Arcuri, L. (2021, March 17). *Learn how to candle an egg*. The Spruce. https://www.thespruce.com/definition-of-candling-3016955

Are chickens really the closest descendants of t-rex? (2017, December 13). Earth Buddies. https://www.earthbuddies.net/are-chickens-really-the-closest-descendants-of-t-rex/

Armitage, N. (2020, February 12). *Dust baths for chickens and what to fill them with*. Cluckin.

https://cluckin.net/dust-baths-for-chickens-and-what-to-fill-them-with.html

B, E. (2016, February 25). *Keeping dogs & chickens.* The Scoop from the Coop. https://www.scoopfromthecoop.com/keeping-dogs-chickens/

Barred rock chickens: complete breed profile. (2021, May 7). The Happy Chicken Coop. https://www.thehappychickencoop.com/barred-rock-chickens-complete-breed-profile/

Belanger, J. D. (2011). *The complete idiot's guide to raising chickens.* Alpha; London.

Biggs, Ph.D., P. (n.d.). *Kids and chickens Tips.* Purina Animal Nutrition. https://www.purinamills.com/chicken-feed/education/detail/backyard-chickens-are-a-kids-best-friend

Black copper marans: complete breed guide. (2021, March 18). www.thehappychickencoop.com. https://www.thehappychickencoop.com/black-copper-marans/

Brock, T. (n.d.). *Tools you need to build a chicken coop.* Dummies. https://www.dummies.com/home-garden/hobby-farming/raising-chickens/tools-you-need-to-build-a-chicken-coop/

Buff orpington all you need to know: temperament and egg laying. (2017, July 24). Thehappychickencoop.com. https://www.thehappychickencoop.com/buff-orpington/

CDC. (2018, May 8). *Outbreaks of human salmonella infections linked to backyard poultry.* Centers for Disease Control and Prevention. https://www.cdc.gov/media/dpk/food-safety/live-poultry-salmonella/live-poultry-salmonella.html

Chicken anatomy 101: everything you need to know. (2018, June 28). Thehappychickencoop.com. https://www.thehappychickencoop.com/chicken-anatomy/

Chicken nesting boxes 101 and 13 best diy plans. (2021, May 26). The Happy Chicken Coop. https://www.thehappychickencoop.com/chicken-nesting-boxes/

Chickens are cool! (50 chicken facts you will love). (n.d.). Backyard Chickens - Learn How to Raise Chickens. https://www.backyardchickens.com/articles/chickens-are-cool-50-chicken-facts-you-will-love.66963/

Cochin chicken: breed profile, care guide and more.... (2017, September 27). Thehappychickencoop.com. https://www.thehappychickencoop.com/cochin-chickens/

Damerow, G. (n.d.). *Raising guinea fowl: a low-maintenance flock.* Mother Earth News.

https://www.motherearthnews.com/homesteading-and-livestock/raising-guinea-fowl-zmaz92aszshe

Damerow, G. (2019, March 22). *How Many Chicken Breeds Are There?* Cackle Hatchery. https://www.cacklehatchery.com/how-many-chicken-breeds-are-there/

Davis, T. (2017a, January 18). *Healthy Herb Garden Chickens Will Love - Top 16 Herbs.* The Imperfectly Happy Home. http://www.imperfectlyhappy.com/herb-garden-chickens/

Davis, T. (2017b, April 10). *Improve the Health of Your Chickens Naturally with 2 Things.* The Imperfectly Happy Home. https://www.imperfectlyhappy.com/chickens-naturally/

Davis, T. (2017c, October 5). *How to have happier chickens - 11 Tips to Make it Easy.* The Imperfectly Happy Home. https://www.imperfectlyhappy.com/how-to-have-happier-chickens/

Do I have to refrigerate my fresh eggs? (n.d.). Fresh Eggs Daily. https://www.fresheggsdaily.blog/2015/09/do-i-have-to-refrigerate-my-fresh-eggs.html

Easter egger: everything you need to know about this chicken. (2021, March 11). The Happy Chicken Coop. https://www.thehappychickencoop.com/easter-egger/

Fulghum, L. (2020, February 24). *How to build a Dropping Board.* Community Chickens.

https://www.communitychickens.com/dropping-board-zb02002ztil/

Hatcher, M. (2010). *Keeping chickens: self-sufficiency.* Skyhorse Publishing.

Hirsch, V. (2003). *Brief summary of the biology and behavior of the chicken.* Animal Legal & Historical Center. www.animallaw.info. https://www.animallaw.info/article/brief-summary-biology-and-behavior-chicken

How much room do chickens need? (2021, March 9). www.thehappychickencoop.com. https://www.thehappychickencoop.com/how-much-room-do-chickens-need/

How to break a broody hen. (n.d.). Fresh Eggs Daily. https://www.fresheggsdaily.blog/2012/01/so-youve-got-broody-hen.html

How to do a chicken health check (checklist included). (n.d.). Www.thehappychickencoop.com. https://www.thehappychickencoop.com/chicken-health-check/

How to prevent and treat the 5 most common chicken diseases. (2019, July 12). Freedom Ranger Blog. https://www.freedomrangerhatchery.com/blog/how-to-prevent-and-treat-the-5-most-common-chicken-diseases/

Jersey giant: size, egg laying, colors, temperament, and more…. (2017, August 19). Thehappychickencoop.com. https://www.thehappychickencoop.com/jersey-giant/

Keene, B. (n.d.). *10 big mistakes first time coop builders make.* Building a Chicken Coop. Retrieved June 25, 2021, from https://www.oregon.gov/ode/students-and-family/childnutrition/F2S/Documents/10mistakes%5B1%5D.pdf

Leghorn chicken: all you need to know. (2021, March 18). www.thehappychickencoop.com. https://www.thehappychickencoop.com/leghorn-chicken/

Leonard, J. (2015, July 14). *20 convincing reasons to keep backyard chickens.* Natural Living Ideas. https://www.naturallivingideas.com/20-convincing-reasons-to-keep-backyard-chickens/

Lockhart, T. (2020, August 13). *The scoop from the coop.* The Scoop from the Coop. https://www.scoopfromthecoop.com/tag/meat-chickens/

Modern Farming Methods. (2015, November 9). *Araucana chicken breed information.* Modern Farming Methods. https://www.roysfarm.com/araucana-chicken/

Niemann, D. (2016, January 18). *11 reasons to keep backyard chickens.* Hobby Farms.

https://www.hobbyfarms.com/11-reasons-to-keep-backyard-chickens/

Peterson, V. J. (2019, May 13). *How to get your chickens to like you.* www.acreagelife.com. https://www.acreagelife.com/hobby-farming/how-to-get-your-chickens-to-like-you

Poindexter, J. (2016, November 14). *How to clean your chicken coop & run: 9 tips to do it right.* MorningChores. https://www.morningchores.com/cleaning-chicken-coop/

Rhode island red: what to know before buying one. (2021, May 4). Thehappychickencoop.com. https://www.thehappychickencoop.com/rhode-island-red/

Rossier, J., & Steele, L. (2017). *Living with chickens: everything you need to know to raise your own backyard flock.* Lyons Press.

Schneider, A. G., & Mccrea, B. (2017). *The chicken whisperer's guide to keeping chickens: everything you need to know-- and didn't know you needed to know about backyard and urban chickens.* Quarry Books.

Shinners, R., & Lowin, R. (2021, January 22). *30 Chicken coop plans that are easy to follow.* Country Living; Country Living. https://www.countryliving.com/diy-crafts/g2452/diy-chicken-coops/

Smith, K. (2013, November 6). *Chicken care and maintenance.* Backyard Chicken Coops. https://www.backyardchickencoops.com.au/blogs/lear ning-centre/chicken-care-maintenance

Smith, K. (2014, March 18). *Natural homemade coop cleaner: citrus, apple cider vinegar, baking powder and more.* Backyard Chicken Coops. https://www.backyardchickencoops.com.au/blogs/lear ning-centre/natural-homemade-chicken-coop-cleaner-orange-peel-white-vinegar

Steele, A.: L. (2021, April 21). *Everything you need to know about chicken roosting bars.* Backyard Poultry. https://www.backyardpoultry.iamcountryside.com/coo ps/chicken-roosting-bars/

Sussex chicken: breed information, care guide, egg color, and more. (2018, March 31). www.thehappychickencoop.com. https://www.thehappychickencoop.com/sussex-chicken/

The egg float test for freshness. (n.d.). Fresh Eggs Daily. https://www.fresheggsdaily.blog/2012/10/the-float-test.html

The plymouth rock chicken: all you need to know. (2021, March 15). www.thehappychickencoop.com. https://www.thehappychickencoop.com/plymouth-rock-chicken/

Thesing, G. (2017, September 13). *Chicken predators – what you need to know.* The Scoop from the Coop.

https://www.scoopfromthecoop.com/chicken-predators-what-you-need-to-know/

Vyse Arks, J. (2021, February 3). *Why keeping chickens is a great idea for families.* Jim Vyse Arks. https://www.jimvysearks.co.uk/why-keeping-chickens-is-a-great-idea-for-families/?doing_wp_cron=1618372147.0487859249114 990234375

What is aspergillosis? plus how to prevent it in your flock. (2019, May 23). Freedom Ranger Blog. https://www.freedomrangerhatchery.com/blog/what-is-aspergillosis-plus-how-to-prevent-it-in-your-flock/

Winger, J. (2020, September 19). *How to build a chicken run.* The Prairie Homestead. https://www.theprairiehomestead.com/2016/08/build-chicken-run.html